THE CANDIDA ALBICANS YEAST-FREE COOKBOOK

About PPNF

Price-Pottenger Nutrition Foundation (PPNF) is a nonprofit educational organization; all contributions and dues are tax-deductible. We trust that you will benefit from the carefully planned diet included herein. When you, as many others have, indicate a desire to help further the work of the Foundation, we urge you to contribute. Please inform others who might also like to take part in facilitating our services to *Candida* patients.

For over thirty years, the Price-Pottenger Nutrition Foundation has kept the work of Weston A. Price, D.D.S., Francis M. Pottenger Jr., M.D., Dr. Melvin Page, and other nutrition professionals available to the public and health professionals. We have seen many nutrition organizations fall by the wayside, their message not received by a public listening only to the allopathic route to "health."

We have prevailed through the years with the support of many determined members. At a time when the public and health providers are looking for answers to the growing decline in the health of Americans, we are now able to contribute our much-needed message. Throughout the years, the Price-Pottenger Nutrition Foundation has maintained a policy to *not compromise our message by taking money for advertising or selling or advocating supplements.* Our foundation exists because of membership support and the sale of books and our materials—*and because our information truly helps people.*

Our catalog of books, reprints, videos, and tapes has been reviewed and approved by PPNF. Most of these books are not the ones you will find on the shelves of the large bookstores! Many of our professional papers, books, and reprints are not available elsewhere.

We invite you to contact us and become a member. Members receive the quarterly *Health and Healing Wisdom Journal*—filled with information that will be helpful to you and your family, a discount of 10 percent on our catalog items, and the referral list for health providers in your state.

We look forward to hearing from you and the opportunity to be of service.

Price-Pottenger Nutrition Foundation
P.O. Box 2617
La Mesa, California 91943-2614
1-619-574-7763
info@price-pottenger.org
www.price-pottenger.org

THE
CANDIDA
ALBICANS
YEAST-FREE
COOKBOOK

How Good Nutrition Can Help Fight the
Epidemic of Yeast-Related Diseases

SECOND EDITION

PAT CONNOLLY
AND THE ASSOCIATES OF THE PRICE-POTTENGER NUTRITION FOUNDATION

FOREWORD BY BEATRICE TRUM HUNTER
INTRODUCTION BY WILLIAM G. CROOK, M.D.

KEATS PUBLISHING

LOS ANGELES

NTC/Contemporary Publishing Group

The information in this book is not intended as medical advice. Its intention is solely informational and educational. It is assumed that the reader will consult a medical or health professional should the need for one be warranted.

Library of Congress Cataloging-in-Publication Data

Connolly, Pat.
    The Candida Albicans yeast-free cookbook : how good nutrition can help fight the epidemic of yeast-related diseases / Pat Connolly and the associates of the Price-Pottenger Nutrition Foundation — 2nd ed.
       p. cm.
    Includes bibliographical references and index.
    ISBN 0-658-00292-9
     1.Candidiasis—Prevention. 2. Candidiasis—Diet therapy—Recipes. 3. Yeast-free diet—Recipes. 4. Sugar-free diet—Recipes. 5. Candida albicans. I. Price-Pottenger Nutrition Foundation. II. Title.

RC123.C3 C66 2000   99-086945
641.5'631—dc21

Published by Keats Publishing
A division of NTC/Contemporary Publishing Group, Inc.
4255 West Touhy Avenue, Lincolnwood, Illinois 60646-1975 U.S.A.

Printed in the United States of America

International Standard Book Number: 0-658-00292-9

  6 7 VRS/VRS 0 4 3

*This book is dedicated to those
who taught us how we should eat:*

Weston A. Price, D.D.S.

Francis M. Pottenger Jr., M.D.

Melvin Page, D.D.S.

Alfreda Rooke, M.P.H.

The Healthy Primitives

Bruce Pacetti, D.D.S.

Joseph Connolly Jr., D.D.S.

Contents

Foreword

Several health problems have burgeoned that appear to be induced by factors in our radical lifestyle transformation. Though disparate, these health problems all seem to be related to imbalances in the body created by replacing novelty foods for traditional ones. We are all participants—with neither knowledge nor consent—to an experiment on an unprecedented scale in the history of humankind. We are eating foods that have been radically altered through various processes of refining, heating, pressurizing, and chemical manipulation. As a result, the food has been disrupted in all classifications of known essential nutrients. The state of the art in food processing has reached a highly sophisticated level. The total sum of the numerous nutrient deficits it produces and their interconnections are difficult to identify. Urbanization along with increased use of medications, alcohol, and drugs further complicate this disruption. There is a glimmer of awareness that some major health problems including cardiovascular diseases, cancer, and schizophrenia seem to be related to dietary alterations.

Candida albicans, quite recently identified as a surprisingly widespread yeast infection, fits this paradigm. The yeast, normally held in check within the healthy body, is out of control and proliferates when the body is in a state of imbalance. Several food and lifestyle factors contribute to making *Candida albicans* a modern problem of epidemic proportions.

Repeated exposures to low levels of antibiotics have succeeded in destroying the beneficial organisms within the human body that normally keep *Candida* in check. Antibiotics are not only administered as medication but also appear in many foods as residue, resulting from their use in food animals. Another factor has been the use of oral contraceptives among women. Steroids, chemical therapies, and numerous drugs, which act as immunosuppressants, weaken the body's ability to maintain balance. Changing dietary patterns, including the increased consumption of simple carbohydrates (refined flours and sugar) at the expense of complex carbohydrates (whole grains or potatoes), provides another opportunity for imbalance.

Imbalance in the body, induced by *Candida*, can be manifested in various organs, tissues, systems, and functions. It may affect the gastrointestinal tract, with symptoms of indigestion, food cravings, or food allergies. Or it may affect the central nervous system, with resultant numbness or tingling. The structure of the body may be affected by joint pains and stiffness. The circulatory system may be impaired, manifested by cold hands and feet. Emotional changes may include fatigue, depression, premenstrual tension, or loss of libido. Hormones may malfunction and result in symptoms running the gamut from acne or dry, rough skin to menstrual disturbances and miscarriage.

Fortunately, once the *Candida* patient is identified, it is possible for the individual to embark on a program to restore the body's balance. Dietary measures are crucial in the control of *Candida*. While identification of *Candida* is probably best done by a health professional, the restoration of health is largely in the hands of the *Candida* sufferer. This cookbook will serve as a reliable guide to help restore the state of balance.

The Rainbow Meal Plan suggested in this book has a good record of effectiveness when used by individuals suffering from a variety of health problems, especially those of fungal origin. The plan can be applied to *Candida* as well. The Rainbow Meal Plan offers good nutrition guidelines but at the same time starves the *Candida*. The underlying principles include traditional foods and avoid novelty ones. Hence, it is reversing long-term detrimental effects. The Modified Meal Plan, a less stringent program than the Rainbow, simply eliminates foods and preparation methods that encourage *Candida*. The recipes follow these rules without sacrificing nutrition or pleasant eating. When faithfully followed, these plans offer hope and restorative possibilities. The ultimate goal is not only to control *Candida albicans* but to balance the body systems properly. With that achievement, good health benefits flow.

—BEATRICE TRUM HUNTER

Preface

It has been fifteen years since this book was first introduced to the public. Since its publication, we have been heartened by the response from our readers and enlightened by the many new introductions to this field of dietary approach to control of yeasts, molds, and fungi.

We have seen many areas of agreement as well as areas of disagreement between *The Candida Albicans Yeast-Free Cookbook* and other *Candida* books on the market. For instance, we are surprised that many of the other cookbooks allow puffed rice cakes and puffed cereals after seeing the research on these "exploded" grains by Paul Stitt, author of *Fighting the Food Giants*. Paul told us that in feeding research, not only were the test animals unable to survive on these puffed grains but they also died sooner than those fed a diet of pure sugar and water. Test animals fed whole grains maintained their health.

We certainly lean even more now toward a low-carbohydrate diet with limited, very occasional use of grains and legumes than we did fifteen years ago. Research by Robert Atkins, M.D., Harold Newbold, M.D., and various anthropologists reminds us that grains and legumes are fairly recent (within the last 8,000 years) introductions to the human diet. Dr. Melvin Page and many other "caveman diet" advocates tell us that this is not long enough for us to adapt to these foods as staples of our diet. Another problem with these foodstuffs is that most of them are highly processed by the time they reach our plates.

We have spoken with patients who have used the Rainbow Diet presented in this book and who have reported that after eating the Rainbow plate of seven, they were still so hungry that they ate 2 cups of beans, or grains, or whatever they liked best. This is *not* what the guidelines call for. If you are still hungry after your plate of six or seven Rainbow foods, you may have equal portions of all seven foods—or six foods if omitting the legume/grain portion—not a binge on the high-carbohydrate portion of the seven. May we suggest that most *Candida* patients can handle one-seventh of their meal in carbohydrate form because it is well-buffered by the five Rainbow vegetables? Today, there are many recommendations from many sources advocating five servings of vegetables each day; this diet has always suggested five servings of a variety of vegetables with each meal or snack.

Researchers at the University of Sydney developed an index based on how full subjects were (their *satiety*) after eating 240 calories' worth of thirty-eight different foods. Potatoes ranked the highest on the satiety index. This means that eating potatoes and sweet potatoes in the carbohydrate portion of our meal can be a great help in avoiding binge gorging to satisfy our hidden hungers. We believe, following the early lead of Orian Truss, M.D., and William Crook, M.D., that everything that goes into your alimentary canal should carry as much nourishment as possible and be low in carbohydrates.

We have been tempted by the suggestion to use vegetable

glycerin as an occasional sweetener but have just seen two articles by Alfreda Way: "Multiple Destruction Through Glycerin—A Hypothesis" and "Glycerin and Disease." These articles made us consider the multitudinous exposures to glycerin we experience in our daily lives, and led us back to the conclusion that the least harmful sweetener is the herb stevia.

Add grapeseed oil to your list of acceptable fats and oils. Jack Tips, N.D., Ph.D., tells us that grapeseed oil is one of the richest sources of linoleic acid, an essential fatty acid; thus, it can nourish many aspects of a person's metabolism and tissue function.

The antifungal qualities of coconut butter have been well expressed by Sally Fallon and Mary Enig, Ph.D., in an article titled "Thailand" from the Human Diets Series, which appeared in volume 22, issue number 4 of the *PPNF Journal:* "But the most protective factor in the Thai diet—and one most ignored by investigators—is the lauric acid found in coconut products. Coconut oil contains almost 50 percent of this twelve-carbon saturated fat, which the body turns into monolaurin, a substance that efficiently kills parasites, yeast, viruses and pathogenic bacteria in the gut."

Preparing your food fresh for each meal can be aided by the use of 4-ounce canning jars for quick one meal/one portion sauces such as salsa; garlic, olive oil, and butter sauce; and so forth. These small 4-ounce jars are available in your grocery store near other canning supplies. They can be used with any blender that will accept a regular-sized canning jar screwed onto its base. Simply cut up your ingredients in the small jar, add the necessary 2 tablespoons of liquid, screw on the rim and blades, place this mini-blender attachment on your blender base, and give it a short swirl to blend your sauce. Try preparing "disguise sauces" to enhance your simple meals, such as mint sauce, raw horseradish, salad dressings, and so forth, which are better made in small portions (in the 4-ounce containers) more frequently. Making small portions more often helps prevent contaminating your leftovers with any molds or yeasts that might accumulate through storing in your refrigerator.

Perhaps the most important addition to the Rainbow Meal Plan is the recognition of Dr. F. Batmanghelidj's valuable research into the severe state of dehydration of most modern people. His book *Your Body's Many Cries for Water* alerts us to the necessity to drink pure water in the ratio of 1 ounce of water for each 2 pounds of body weight each day. This translates to 64 ounces of water, or 2 quarts of water, for a 128-pound person. Sheba Penner suggests drinking a glass of water each time that we urinate to replenish our fluid balance. It is best to drink the major portion of our water in between, before, and after meals, rather than during meals.

WHY WE USE AS MUCH RAW FOOD AS POSSIBLE

Francis Marion Pottenger Jr., M.D., conducted a ten-year research project with over 900 cats comparing the health of cats fed raw food with that of cats fed two-thirds of their diet cooked. If these results are comparable to human responses to diet, a startling bit of evidence reminds us to incorporate as much raw food into our diets as possible. The cats fed raw food were healthy, while those fed cooked food degenerated more in each generation. The third generation of cats fed cooked foods did not live long enough to reproduce. For each vegetable that you make part of your Rainbow meal, do decide if the preparation of that food enhances or detracts from its food value. Should you eat it raw? Are you going to bite off a bit and chew it, shred it, julienne it, or lightly steam it?

When you choose a cooked recipe from this book, always add as much raw vegetable food to the meal as possible to supply the vital live-food factors such as enzymes and other heat-labile factors. Usually, this adds some "crunch," which both satisfies the appetite and enhances the production of salivary digestive factors.

Dr. Cass Ingram has shared with us his top twelve supermarket remedies to inhibit *Candida*. Do try to include as many of the following foods from his list as possible in your daily Rainbow meal plans.

1. Avocado contains antifungal fatty acids and is sugar-free.
2. Basil contains antifungal volatile oils.
3. Beef contains curative factors of selenium and amino acids.
4. Chicken and chicken soup are good media to deliver garlic broth.
5. Cumin has antifungal essential oils.
6. Garlic is a natural antifungal agent.
7. Ginger root has antiseptic enzymes and oils.
8. Horseradish has antiseptic enzymes and oils.
9. Onion is antifungal and provides sulfur.
10. Oregano has potent antifungal activity due to its antimicrobial volatile oils.
11. Radishes contain selenium, sulfur, and antibiotics.
12. He also mentions the use of yogurt, although yogurt recipes are not included in this cookbook.

This Rainbow Diet was designed to remove foods that interfere with healing from your eating plan and to emphasize foods that build health. Your diet should be fresh, natural, simple to prepare, and nourishing, once you have removed the foods that encourage yeast proliferation. Some users have called it a "natural healing diet." We are confident that you'll come to the same conclusion.

Acknowledgments

We wish to thank the many who helped make this book possible:

The *Candida* patients who insisted on dietary help in book form.

Shirley Lorenzani, who first told us of the yeast problem.

Bruce Pacetti, who refined Price and Page dietary ideas into the Rainbow Meal Plan.

An Keats, whose patience and help made her a joy to work with.

Mary Marston, who experienced the diet; wrote detailed instructions for us; and researched, tested, and rewrote recipes.

Nancy Kelly, who kept us going day after day and pulled it all together.

Arthur Mitchell, who brought us reference cookbooks at critical times.

William G. Crook, M.D., who cheerfully gave us valuable advice.

C. Orian Truss, M.D., and his team of hundreds of physicians who are showing us how to regain our health.

Helen Fahrney, who tasted, made suggestions, and tasted again.

Introduction

Do you feel bad all over? Are you bothered with fatigue, headaches, depression, irritability, and memory loss? Or do you suffer symptoms caused by disturbances in your reproductive organs, including prostatitis, loss of sexual interest and/or impotence, premenstrual tension, menstrual irregularities, persistent vaginitis, endometriosis, or infertility?

Are you troubled with digestive symptoms, sore muscles and joints, multiple sclerosis, chronic hives, psoriasis (or other skin problems), or mitral valve prolapse? If your answer is "yes" to any of these questions and if you've taken antibiotics, oral contraceptives, or corticosteroids, chances are that your health problems are related to the common and usually benign yeast *Candida albicans*.

For centuries, this yeast has been known to cause vaginal problems and skin and mouth rashes. However, not until the brilliant pioneer observations of C. Orian Truss, M.D., did physicians (or anyone else) realize that this usually benign "critter" could play an important part in causing so many health problems.

Some thirty years ago, Truss, a Birmingham, Alabama, internist and allergist, first noted that *Candida albicans* made several of his patients sick. During the next sixteen years, he saw many other patients whose illnesses were related to yeasts. He reported his findings in a series of four articles in the *Journal of Orthomolecular Psychiatry* beginning in 1978. Yet prior to 1982, only a handful of physicians had learned of his observations.

Then, beginning in 1982, word of the yeast-human relationship began to spread. Now, hundreds of physicians and tens of thousands of yeast victims are learning about yeast-connected health disorders.

I first became aware of Truss's work in 1979, and since then, I've seen hundreds of patients respond to antifungal medication and a sugar-free, yeast-free diet.

You are what you eat, and eating really nutritious food is your most important requirement for good health. Yet in the United States today, you're constantly encouraged by television and media advertising to eat processed, sweetened, colored, and refined foods. Moreover, some nutrition "authorities" even endorse the consumption of such foods.

But there are dissenting voices—courageous, knowledge-able, and articulate individuals who are "telling it like it is" and working to bring sound nutritional knowledge to all who would listen. One such individual is Pat Connolly, Curator of the Price-Pottenger Nutrition Foundation. During the past decade, I've learned a lot from Pat's clinical observations and from the publications of the Price-Pottenger Foundation.

If you're bothered by yeast-connected health problems, you'll need the help, support, and encouragement of an experi-enced and interested physician and other health professionals to prescribe antifungal medication and to supervise your overall treatment program. Equally important, you'll need to consume a well-balanced, nutritious diet composed of foods that don't encourage yeast growth.

Yeasts thrive on carbohydrates, especially foods that contain sugar. Accordingly, you'll need to avoid all foods containing table sugar and refined forms of sucrose, glucose, and fructose. In addition, during the initial weeks on your diet, you'll need to avoid fruits and you may also need to avoid the high-carbohydrate grains, especially those containing gluten. You'll also need to avoid mushrooms, cheeses, and other yeast-containing foods since many individuals with yeast-related health problems experience allergic reactions when they eat these foods. As your immune system improves and the *Candida* in your digestive tract is brought under control, your diet can usually be expanded.

The Candida Albicans Yeast-Free Cookbook provides a dietary program that has been found to be highly effective in bringing *Candida* overgrowth in the digestive tract under control. Featured are many recipes that will help you maintain an adequate nutritional state while starving the *Candida* organisms that live in your digestive tract. Although the initial phases of the program are rigorous and demanding, as you improve you can usually return some of these forbidden foods to your diet, including the complex carbohydrates.

Bringing the yeast-connected health disorder under control and regaining your health won't be easy. It usually requires months and years of patient, consistent work. This book should help you significantly in regaining your health.

—WILLIAM G. CROOK, M.D.

Do You Have *Candida Albicans?*

A QUESTIONNAIRE

The remarkable recovery of many patients suffering from the symptoms associated with *Candida albicans* and the development of this cookbook are mainly due to the efforts of two medical doctors who have persisted courageously in research that has brought *Candida albicans* to the forefront of current medical issues. C. Orian Truss, M.D., of Birmingham, Alabama, and Sidney M. Baker, M.D., of The Gesell Institute of Human Behavior, New Haven, Connecticut, are recognized pioneers in current research and clinical observations of yeast-connected illnesses.

In his enlightening book *The Missing Diagnosis,* Dr. Truss cites numerous cases of misdiagnosed, untreated *Candida* patients who were often stigmatized as psychosomatics.[1] According to Dr. Truss, "*Candida albicans* is in everyone and it is readily apparent that its presence is entirely compatible with a lifetime of excellent health. It is equally apparent, however, that under the influence of various factors, it may successfully invade and colonize mucous membranes, skin and nails.... Such infections may be acute, brief, and intermittent."

Truss's work is of major significance in that he has

documented histories of patients with a wide spectrum of symptoms who have drastically improved or completely recovered under his treatment program for *Candida*, which includes dietary restraints and often the use of nystatin.

He cautions, however, that these remarkable recoveries may in fact be related to some aspect of the treatment plan other than the "die-off" of the fungi. "Even should *Candida* be unrelated etiologically, patients with an autoimmune disease deserve to have their yeast problems treated. If it is not the cause of their illness, treating it should do no harm, and if it is the cause, then that is what we are looking for," Truss concluded in his paper, "The Role of *Candida Albicans* in Human Illness."[2]

With the growing awareness of *Candida* as a systemic illness that plays a significant role in health, the question arises: Why has it not been discussed in medical journals for so long? Dr. Truss believes that there are two reasons. At present, definitive tests are nonexistent for identification of *Candida* as a causative indicator, since it is present in most individuals and is often categorized as an "opportunistic organism." Also, what Dr. Truss calls the "psychosomatic complex" has provided a safety valve for doctors who attempt to diagnose patients' complaints that have no clearly discernible cause.

According to Dr. Truss, the proliferation of broad-spectrum antibiotics following World War II and, later, the widespread use of both birth control pills and cortisone-type steroids, combined with increasingly high-carbohydrate diets, has culminated in numerous yeast-related illnesses. He suggests that current problems, including drug abuse, behavioral disorders, and suicide among young people, may be related to an inefficiently functioning immune system and the consequences of *Candida albicans* overgrowth.

In recent years, medical researchers of *Candida albicans*-related syndromes have pooled their findings at several national conferences. At the Yeast-Human-Interaction Conference in November 1983, Drs. Truss and Baker were featured speakers.

The Yeast Connection: A Medical Breakthrough, by William G. Crook, M.D., published in 1983, is a guidebook for patients and the general public that provides a better understanding of the implications and complications in diagnosis and treatment of *Candida albicans.*[3]

The following questionnaire, designed by Dr. Crook, provides a list of the symptoms and medical histories that might indicate the presence of *Candida* overgrowth. The variety of symptoms, however, suggests the importance of making the diagnosis with a physician's guidance.

Candida Questionnaire and Score Sheet

This questionnaire is designed for adults and is not appropriate for children. It lists factors in your medical history that promote the growth of *Candida albicans* (Section A) and symptoms commonly found in individuals with yeast-connected illnesses (Sections B and C).

For each "Yes" answer in Section A, circle the Point Score in that section. Total your score and record it in the box at the end of the section. Then move on to Sections B and C and score as directed.

Filling out and scoring this questionnaire should help you and your physician evaluate the possible role of *Candida* in contributing to your health problem, but it will not provide an absolute "Yes" or "No" answer.

Section A | **History**   **Point Score**

1. Have you taken tetracyclines (Sumycin®,
    Panmycin®, Vibramycin®, Minocin®, etc.) or other
    antibiotics for acne for 1 month (or longer)? 35

2. Have you, at any time in your life, taken other
    "broad-spectrum" antibiotics† for respiratory,
    urinary, or other infections (for two months or
    longer, or in shorter courses 4 or more times in a
    1-year period)? 35

3. Have you taken a broad-spectrum antibiotic
    drug*—even a single course? 6

4. Have you, at any time in your life, been bothered
    by persistent prostatitis, vaginitis, or other prob-
    lems affecting your reproductive organs? 25

5. Have you been pregnant
    2 or more times? 5
    1 time? 3

6. Have you taken birth control pills
    For more than 2 years? 15
    For 6 months to 2 years? 8

7. Have you taken prednisone, Decadron®, or other
    cortisone-type drugs
    For more than 2 weeks? 15
    For 2 weeks or less? 6

---

* Including Keflex®, ampicillin, amoxicillin, Ceclor®, Bactrim®, and Septra®. Such
antibiotics kill off "good germs" while they're killing off those that cause infection.

8. Does exposure to perfumes, insecticides,   **Point Score**
    fabric shop odors, and other chemicals provoke
    Moderate to severe symptoms? 20
    Mild symptoms? 5

9. Are your symptoms worse on damp, muggy days,
    or in moldy places? 20

10. Have you had athlete's foot, ringworm, "jock itch," or
    other chronic fungus infections of the skin or nails?
    Have such infections been
    Severe or persistent? 20
    Mild to moderate? 10

11. Do you crave sugar? 10

12. Do you crave breads? 10

13. Do you crave alcoholic beverages? 10

14. Does tobacco smoke *really* bother you? 10

Total Score, *Section A* .... _____

Section B | **Major Symptoms**

For each of your symptoms, enter the appropriate figure
in the Point Score column:

If a symptom is occasional or mild .... score 3 points

If a symptom is frequent and/or
moderately severe .... score 6 points

If a symptom is severe and/or disabling .... score 9 points

Add total score and record it in the box at the end of this section

Point Score

1. Fatigue or lethargy .... _____

2. Feeling of being "drained" .... _____

3. Poor memory .... _____

4. Feeling "spacey" or "unreal" .... _____

5. Inability to make decisions .... _____

6. Numbness, burning, or tingling .... _____

7. Insomnia .... _____

8. Muscle aches .... _____

9. Muscle weakness or paralysis .... _____

10. Pain and/or swelling in joints .... _____

11. Abdominal pain .... _____

12. Constipation .... _____

13. Diarrhea .... _____

14. Bloating, belching, or intestinal gas .... _____

15. Troublesome vaginal burning,
    itching, or discharge .... _____

16. Prostatitis .... _____

17. Impotence .... _____

18. Loss of sexual desire or feeling .... _____

19. Endometriosis or infertility .... _____

20. Cramps and/or other menstrual irregularities ...... _____

21. Premenstrual tension .... _____

22. Attacks of anxiety or crying .... _____

23. Cold hands or feet and/or chilliness .... _____

24. Shaking or irritable when hungry .... _____

Total Score, *Section B* .... _____

A Questionnaire

Section C | **Other Symptoms**†

For each of your symptoms, enter the appropriate figure in the Point Score column:

If a symptom is occasional or mild .... score 1 point

If a symptom is frequent and/or
moderately severe .... score 2 points

If a symptom is severe and/or disabling .... score 3 points

Add total score and record it in the box at the end of this section.

Point Score

1. Drowsiness .... _____
2. Irritability or jitteriness .... _____
3. Incoordination .... _____
4. Inability to concentrate .... _____
5. Frequent mood swings .... _____
6. Headache .... _____
7. Dizziness/loss of balance .... _____
8. Pressure above ears; feeling of head swelling ...... _____
9. Tendency to bruise easily .... _____
10. Chronic rashes or itching .... _____
11. Numbness, tingling .... _____
12. Indigestion or heartburn .... _____
13. Food sensitivity or intolerance .... _____
14. Mucus in stools .... _____
15. Rectal itching .... _____

---

† While the symptoms in this section commonly occur in people with yeast-connected illness, they are also found in other individuals.

16. Dry mouth or throat .... _____

17. Rash or blisters in mouth .... _____

18. Bad breath .... _____

19. Foot, hair, or body odor not relieved by washing .. _____

20. Nasal congestion or post-nasal drip .... _____

21. Nasal itching .... _____

22. Sore throat .... _____

23. Laryngitis, loss of voice .... _____

24. Cough or recurrent bronchitis .... _____

25. Pain or tightness in chest .... _____

26. Wheezing or shortness of breath .... _____

27. Urinary urgency or frequency .... _____

28. Burning on urination .... _____

29. Spots in front of eyes or erratic vision .... _____

30. Burning or tearing of eyes .... _____

31. Recurrent infections or fluid in ears .... _____

32. Ear pain or deafness .... _____

Total Score, *Section C* .... _____

Total Score, *Section B* .... _____

Total Score, *Section A* .... _____

Grand Total Score .... _____

The Grand Total Score will help you and your physician decide if your health problems are yeast-connected. Scores in women will run higher as 7 items in the questionnaire apply exclusively to women, while only 2 apply exclusively to men.

A Questionnaire

Yeast-connected health problems are almost certainly present in women with scores *over 180* and in men with scores *over 140*.

Yeast-connected health problems are probably present in women with scores *over 120* and in men with scores *over 90*.

Yeast-connected health problems are possibly present in women with scores *over 60* and in men with scores *over 40*.

With scores of less than 60 in women and 40 in men, yeasts are less apt to cause health problems.

This questionnaire is reproduced with the kind permission of William G. Crook, M.D., and is available from Professional Books, P.O. Box 3494, Jackson, Tennessee 38301. Prices on request. *The Yeast Connection*, copyright © 1983 by William G. Crook, M.D.

Living with
Candida Albicans

Shopping, Planning, and Using Leftovers

A fully effective diet for the treatment of *Candida* must not only starve the yeast but provide all essential nutrients needed for the healing process. To promote adherence to the diet, meals should be satisfying, attractive, tasty, and simple to prepare. The suggested diet is one that emphasizes a variety of vegetables and small amounts of protein; it also includes legumes and some grains. All foods should be fresh and whole. Conspicuously absent in the beginning of the program are fruits; honey; dairy products; seeds and nuts;* and yeasted and fermented foods. Although these are wholesome foods, they do not retard the growth of *Candida*.

---

* When symptoms abate, your doctor will reintroduce seeds and grains into the diet. Usually portions are restricted to ⅛ or ¼ cup of sprouted seeds or grains. Non-yeasted bread may be substituted in the same amount. Be sure to measure. If this amount is well tolerated, repeat again in four days. If no problems arise, add this amount of the new food to your diet. Use the same process of four-day testing for additional nuts and grains. Wait six weeks before repeating a test food if it is not well tolerated.

Sugar in *any* form, including fruit, honey, molasses, maple syrup, and all alcoholic beverages, makes *Candida* thrive and must be avoided. Since milk products contain milk sugar (lactose), all dairy foods except butter must also be omitted. Seeds and nuts are initially excluded because they are difficult to digest. They may be reinstated into the diet by trial and error experimentation at a later date.*

Yeast-containing foods, such as vinegar, mushrooms, yeasted breads, beer, wine, and brewer's yeast must all be avoided. The *Candida* patient is already reacting to the *Candida* overgrowth in the body. Yeast-containing foods add an overload to the immune system, which is already functioning inefficiently.

Once you understand the simple basic principles of creating a yeast-free diet, you can enjoy attractive and nutritious meals that will help hasten your recovery from annoying chronic symptoms. Two varied and appetizing meal plans are presented to offer you satisfying meals and help you treat *Candida* effectively. The Rainbow Meal Plan is a clinically tested healing regimen for balancing the body's chemistry, which is under stress from *Candida* and possibly from other factors.

The Modified Meal Plan is a collection of tested recipes that make use of the basic foods acceptable in an antifungal diet. You can choose the meal plan that best suits your needs and tastes. Or you can alternate plans while you work to restore your health and vigor.

Anti-Candida Shopping

For the yeast-free special diet or the yeast-free low-carbohydrate diet plans, supermarket shopping is easier than ever before. In general, you can bypass about 80 percent of the foods offered, and head directly to a few sections:

Meats: Select fresh lean meats, poultry, and fish. Avoid ground meat, pork, breaded and pickled meats, or any processed meat with additives. Some frozen food can be stored for convenience—for instance, keep a bag of frozen (unbreaded) scallops on hand. It's so easy to thaw a few for a quick meal, and reseal the package.
Dairy Products: Select fresh eggs and unsalted butter and ignore the rest. Look for the date on the egg cartons.
Seeds, Nuts, Legumes, and Grains: These may be found in bulk packages. Be sure to use brown rice and whole grains.
Produce: Pass up the fruit section. Select vegetables that look fresh and free of mold.
Condiments: Select olive oil, spices, herbs, and sea salt.
Canned Goods: A few canned goods (without additives), such as tomato paste, water chestnuts, olives, tuna, and sardines, are acceptable for emergencies. Choose canned tomato products without citric acid.
Frozen Vegetables: Stock some, such as frozen artichoke hearts or green peas, for soups and salads. Check labels and avoid those with sugar, vinegar, and additives.
Deli Section: Select corn tortillas and shun everything else. Check the label carefully to avoid preservatives, and inspect package for mold.
Crackers: If you can't find yeast- and sugar-free whole grain crackers in the supermarket, look for them in the health food store.
Caution: Don't overbuy! Purchase fresh foods frequently, as soon as possible after they are delivered to the store.

Health/Natural Food Stores

Although you can purchase most of your yeast-free foods at regular supermarkets, health/natural food stores are good sources of high-quality foods such as olive oil, raw butter, and fertile eggs. It is as necessary to scrutinize labels in these stores as it is in supermarkets, for not all produce is organic, nor are all meats free from additives. Now that unsafe levels of EDB (ethylene dibromide), a carcinogenic fumigant, have been found in many foods (including high levels in grains and flours), choosing organic, unfumigated grain is more important than ever.

 Yeast-free crackers, breads, and tortillas are commonly available at health/natural food stores. Select beans you have never tried before, such as azuki beans, or experiment with fresh herbs as well as specialty grains such as millet and brown rice. Be careful, however, of any packaged goods that claim to be "sugar free." Read label ingredients carefully, for usually the contents do include sweeteners. "Sugar free" is a misnomer, denoting only sucrose (table sugar). Most prepared and processed foods and

Recommended foods	Foods to be avoided
lean fresh meats, including beef and lamb	sugar in all forms, including honey and molasses
all forms of fowl	dairy products, except butter
organ meats	white flour products
fresh game meat	seeds and nuts (see page 11)
deep-sea fish	yeast- and mold-containing foods (see pages 201–202);
vegetables	
greens	vinegar, mushrooms, sauerkraut, cheeses
roots	prepared sauces such as soy sauce
complex starches in limited quantities: legumes and grains	
	juices
water: pure, mineral	food additives, including citric acid
fats and oils: olive oil, butter	fruit

many vitamin supplements contain yeast. Again, *read labels carefully*. It is best to make dressings and sauces from scratch and use fresh ingredients.

Planning: A Key Factor

One key to success in using these diets is to plan ahead. When hunger strikes, it is all too easy to reach into the refrigerator and grab the first thing available. Haphazard eating will not assure balance and necessary nutrient intake. Plan your day to include time for preparation of meals. This will help you adhere to your diet guidelines and speed the healing process.

Plan to keep one or two individual portions of a cooked meat or soup in the freezer. Then you can select a package to use at home or to take out with you, and allow it to defrost en route.

If you are planning to be away from home all day, take along small snacks or a meal to avoid being caught hungry without your allowed foods.

Freezing Leftovers

Refrigerated food deteriorates in quality very rapidly. It also supports the growth of bacteria and mold. To prevent this, freeze all unused portions of meals that you wish to save each day to use at a later date. Uncooked meat, poultry, or seafood should be frozen until the day you plan to prepare it. F. Granville Knight, M.D., author of *Physical Degeneration and Allergy* and *What Are Pesticides Doing to Human Beings?*, in personal conversations repeatedly stated that freezing and thawing meats caused about a 20 percent loss of nutrients, which he felt was a good trade-off if one could obtain better-quality meats through frozen storage. Small quantities of freshly cooked beans and grains are always best, but in emergencies, larger quantities can be cooked and divided into individual portions to be frozen. An easy way to ensure quick defrosting is to freeze single portions in heavy plastic bags. Distribute the contents evenly. (Blocks of food take more time to defrost.) Freeze any leftovers from your recipes to prevent growth of molds and bacteria.

THE RAINBOW MEAL PLAN

Price-Page-Pacetti Diet

Weston A. Price, D.D.S., a nutritional pioneer in the 1920s, observed eating patterns of healthy people throughout remote areas of the world. He attributed their optimal health to diets derived from indigenous whole foods, high in minerals, vitamins, dietary fiber, essential fatty acids, and an unidentified element he termed "Factor X." This mysterious factor was found to be a catalyst that enhances mineral absorption and assimilation. Price found it in environments as varied as the northern tundra and tropical rain forests. Price's work has been preserved in his classic text, *Nutrition and Physical Degeneration,* which includes photographic documentation of his findings.[4]

Dr. Melvin Page, also a dentist, was a colleague and protégé of Dr. Price. Having studied the Price research, he applied the findings to his patients. He advised them to avoid all refined foods, especially sugar. He found, through precise laboratory analyses, that when patients ate sugar and other refined foods, their blood chemistries became abnormal. When they followed a diet of fresh vegetables, whole grains, and protein, their blood chemistries shifted toward normal.[5]

The Rainbow Meal Plan*

① Complete Protein
beef, chicken, crustaceans, duck, eggs, fish, lamb, mollusks, turkey

⑦ Green Leafy Vegetables
beet tops, bok choy, brussels sprouts, cabbage, Chinese cabbage, collard greens, endive, kale, Bibb lettuce, leafy lettuce, romaine lettuce, mustard greens, parsley, spinach, Swiss chard, turnip greens, watercress

② Legumes & Grains
beans: azuki, black-eyed, kidney, lentil, lima, navy, pinto, soy, string
peas: chick, green, snap, snow
whole grains: barley, brown rice, buckwheat, millet, oats, rye, wheat berries

Pure water

③ Root Vegetables
beets, carrots, Jerusalem artichokes, onions, parsnips, potatoes, rutabagas, turnips

⑥ Red, Orange, Purple Vegetables
beets, carrots, eggplant, pumpkin, red cabbage, red peppers, butternut squash, sweet potatoes, tomatoes

④ Yellow or White Vegetables
cauliflower, fresh corn, cucumbers, onions, parsnips, radish, rutabagas, acorn squash, hubbard squash, turnips

⑤ Green Vegetables
artichokes, asparagus, broccoli, celery, endive, green pepper, kohlrabi, leeks, okra, scallions, snap peas, snow peas, string beans, zucchini

*Reproduced with the kind permission of the Page Foundation.

Homeostasis, the scientific word for internal balance, is the state of healthy blood chemistry observed by Dr. Page. In this steady, balanced state, humans can find health. In this state, the body maintains blood pressure, blood sugar, body temperature, and other functions within a non-stressful range.

Homeostasis, the steady state of man, comes as part of our human heritage. We are equipped with systems, backup systems, and emergency generators to maintain internal equilibrium.

Stress, from food, emotions, lack of rest, injury, or nutritional deficiencies, can upset the equilibrium. The body can deal with occasional stress very efficiently. It's when stress becomes continuous that the body's balancing act is difficult, if not impossible, to maintain.

Dr. Page observed that stress from food was a powerful insult to the body's equilibrium. Sugar was found to be the prime offender. Laboratory analyses showed that some Page patients experienced upset blood chemistry for four days after eating sugars. This included honey, molasses, and syrups. On the basis of these studies, Dr. Page recommended no refined sugars or even fruits during periods of recovery from illness. During times of health, he recommended only occasional desserts and fruit.

Another dentist and nutritionist, Bruce Pacetti, has made exciting contributions and additions to the work begun by Drs. Price and Page. Dr. Pacetti has observed that many patients with chronic health problems, especially candidiasis, have developed sensitivities or allergies to foods. Their digestive systems are not working efficiently. When foods are not digested completely, toxins are produced in the intestines and then absorbed into the bloodstream. Incomplete digestion also means that valuable nutrients are not being absorbed from foods. All this—toxins and lack of nutrients—contributes to tipping the internal balance to imbalance. Lack of homeostasis, our steady internal state, prevents healing. To allow for better digestion, reduce the allergic reaction to foods, and provide a wide range of essential vitamins, minerals, and enzymes, Dr. Pacetti has developed the Rainbow Meal Plan. This beautiful, colorful array of vegetables, whole grains, and protein offers a variety of textures, tastes, and nutrients. Possible allergic reactions are minimized by eating only a small portion of each item. The effectiveness of the Rainbow Meal Plan for *Candida* patients is corroborated by Shirley S. Lorenzani, Ph.D., author of *Candida: A Twentieth-Century Disease* (Los Angeles: Keats Publishing, 1986), whose articles, lectures and tapes have inspired thousands of other *Candida* patients to modify their eating habits and once again enjoy good health.[6]

The Rainbow Plate includes small portions of seven food groups: complete protein; grain or legume; root vegetable; yellow or white vegetable; green vegetable; red, orange, or purple vegetable; and green leafy vegetable.

An extremely ill person with poorly functioning digestion will want to begin with very small portions, as small as an eighth of a cup of each item. Such a person may need to eat many small meals each day. Eating every two hours may be necessary until digestion improves.

Others may eat larger portions. There is no need to measure your portions meticulously. You may want to use a measuring cup or spoon at first, but soon you can estimate accurately. It is easy to determine when your portion sizes have become too large. If you feel full after eating, you ate too much. The ideal Rainbow Plate will leave you feeling light and comfortable.

Why not begin by eating very small portions? If that works for you, continue until your body demands larger portions.

Remember to keep all items approximately the same size. Have the same amount of green leafy vegetables as you do grains or beans.

Complete guidelines for the Rainbow Meal Plan are as follows:

1. Prepare and eat small portions (these may range from an eighth to a quarter of a cup of *each* of the seven categories in the beginning).
2. Choose one food from each category.
3. All vegetables should be raw or gently steamed, not overcooked.
4. Kelp powder, Celtic sea salt, plain pepper, and raw butter can be used in moderation.
5. Digestion begins in your mouth. Chew thoroughly and enjoy every bite.
6. Drink only pure water. Sip small amounts with meals and drink at least eight glasses a day between meals.
7. Eat as many meals per day as desired. Use these meals for a snack; conform to these guidelines and space your meals at least two hours apart.
8. To aid digestion, relax before, during, and after your meals. Keep your thoughts and conversation calm.

This meal plan is satisfying in many ways. Once you have become familiar with shopping for a variety of foods, storing them conveniently, and cooking with a steamer, it will be easy and delightful. If variety is the spice of life, there is no question that it is the spice of eating! Taste buds will soon anticipate the many tastes and textures on the Rainbow Plate. Cells will appreciate the many vitamins, minerals, and enzymes.

What to do when you eat out? Salad bars and lightly cooked vegetables and proteins provide a simple solution. Sharing an entrée with a friend is often a way to economize for your health and finances. Protein portions in most restaurants are more than adequate for two people.

Can you take a Rainbow Meal to work? Certainly. Just prepare several meals at breakfast and pack one or two for your time away from home. Soups and stews containing foods from the seven groups are a delicious and simple way to eat on the job. A large thermos can provide several meals.

While many people experience the Rainbow Meal Plan as a satisfying, orderly, disciplined way of eating, others interpret it as too structured, too demanding. If you find yourself spending too much time planning and preparing for meals, shift to the Modified Food Plan featured in this book. The carbohydrate content of each recipe as well as the chart on pages 204–211 are tools for the reader taking a physician's advice to follow a diet low in carbohydrates. Dr. Crook notes that the amount for each person can vary as much as 100 grams daily, so be sure to consult your personal physician about your diet.[7] You may also choose to eat some of your meals from the Rainbow Plan and others from the Modified Plan. You might eat breakfast from the Modified Food Plan and enjoy a Rainbow Plate for lunch and dinner. Both the Rainbow Plate and the Modified Food Plan are excellent styles of eating that can give you the dietary support necessary to regain abundant health. You may also lightly season your food with sea salt, particularly that from the Brittany seacoast. According to Dr. Jacques de Langre:

The minerals that are contained in real sea salt are the eighty-four elements that are originally in the sea. When these elements are removed, as in the case of white table salt and all so-called "sea salt," the body starves. Salt is such an important part of our food that very close scrutiny, attention, and sensitivity must be given to the method used to produce it, so that the end product accurately fits our biological requirements. To determine if a salt is a truly whole product of natural crystallization of the ocean, use the following guidelines: Authentic natural sea salt (1) is light gray in color and on standing, the color darkens slightly at the base of the container; (2) is moist to the touch and remains moist even when kept in cool storage for long periods; and (3) is formed of small, precisely cubic crystals.

Select equal portions from the following seven food categories:

Complete Protein			
one			
MEATS			
• beef	• frog legs	• kidney	• sweetbreads
• beef brains	• gelatin, plain	• lamb	• veal
• beef heart	(incomplete	• liver	• wild (squirrel,
• beef tongue	protein)	• mutton	deer)
• buffalo	• goat meat	• rabbit	
	• goose		
FOWL			
• chicken	• goose	• organ meats	• pheasant
• duck		(from chicken,	• turkey
		turkey, etc.)	

Complete Protein *continued*

one

EGGS

- chicken
- duck
- goose

FISH, MOLLUSKS, AND CRUSTACEANS

• abalone	• crayfish	• mullet (Lisa)	• shrimp
• anchovy	• fish roe	• oysters	• smelt
• bass	• flounder	• perch	• sole
• carp	• haddock	• pompano	• sunfish
• caviar	• halibut	• red snapper	• swordfish
• clam	• herring	• salmon	• tuna
• cod	• lobster	• sardine	• whitefish
• crab	• mackerel	• scallop	• whiting
• crappie	(Spanish)	• shark	

two

GRAINS

• amaranth	• flaxseed	• psyllium seed husks	• sprouted grains (barley, wheat, rye)
• barley	• millet	• quinoa	• teff
• buckwheat	• oats	• rice (brown)	
• corn	• oat bran		

LEGUMES

beans	• lima	• string	*peas*
• azuki	• mung	• black-eyed	• chick garbanzos
• black	• navy	*lentils*	• snap
• kidney	• pinto		• split

Vegetables

three

ROOT VEGETABLES

• anise root	• celeriac (celery root)	• parsnip	• radish
• beet	• Jerusalem artichokes	• parsley root	• rutabaga
• carrot	• onion	• Irish potato	• turnip
		• sweet potato	• yam

Vegetables *continued*

four

YELLOW AND WHITE VEGETABLES

- avocado
- bean sprouts, mung
- beans, wax
- cauliflower
- corn
- cucumber
- endive, Belgian
- jicama
- onion
- parsnip
- radish
- rutabaga
- squash (yellow, crook-necked)
- turnip

five

GREEN VEGETABLES

- artichoke, globe
- asparagus
- bean, lima
- beans, string
- broccoli
- celery
- kohlrabi
- leeks
- okra
- olive
- pea pods (edible)
- peas, green
- peas, sugar snap
- pepper, green
- sprouts
- scallions
- zucchini

six

RED, ORANGE, AND PURPLE VEGETABLES

- beets
- carrots
- eggplant
- pumpkin
- red cabbage
- red bell peppers
- sweet potato
- tomato
- winter squash
- yam

seven

LEAFY GREEN VEGETABLES

- artichokes, globe
- beet tops
- bok choy
- brussels sprouts
- cabbage
- chicory
- chives
- cilantro
- collards
- dandelion
- endive
- escarole
- kale
- lettuce, iceberg
- lettuce, red leaf
- lettuce, romaine
- mustard greens
- parsley
- spinach
- summer savory
- turnip greens
- watercress
- Swiss chard
- sunflower greens

TYPICAL RAINBOW RECIPES

A Rainbow Breakfast

A Rainbow Meal can be used for breakfast, but if you feel like a more traditional meal, you might enjoy the egg combinations below.

Equipment needed	Stainless steel pot: 2- or 3-quart size with lid
	Stainless steel steamer basket
	Pyrex custard cup
	Cutting board with sharp knife
Complete protein	1 raw egg, in the shell
Starch	¼ cup cooked brown rice
Root vegetable	¼ cup raw shredded beets or carrots
White vegetable	¼ cup onions, chopped
Green vegetable	¼ cup celery, chopped
Red vegetable	1 medium tomato, finely chopped
Leafy green vegetable	Parsley, coarsely chopped

Place steamer basket and ½ inch water in pot. Place whole egg in the steamer basket, cover the pot, and bring water to boil. Reduce heat to medium and set timer for 6 minutes. Put cooked rice (in custard cup) in pot beside egg. (Re-cover the pot after each addition.) After 2 minutes, add beets or carrots and onions. After 2 additional minutes, add celery. After another 2 minutes, add tomato and parsley. Remove the egg from the pan when the timer says 6 to 7 minutes; hold the egg under running cold water briefly to stop the cooking process. Crack open the egg onto the plate or into an egg cup. Dividing the plate into three areas, serve the beats or carrots on the second area, the rice on the third. Scoop the remaining vegetables over the egg and over the rice, as desired. Add a pat of butter and season. Serves 1.

Note: In general, denser foods, such as meats and root vegetables, are added at the beginning of the cooking process, the more delicate foods later. If necessary, lift the lid from time to time and remove cooked vegetables that have reached a brilliant color to avoid overcooking.

Note: The carbohydrate contents for all recipes are approximate and are based on analyses of the dishes as prepared; thus variations in carbohydrate values for the same amounts of the same ingredients will be noticed. This range of variation depends on seasonal changes in foods, differences among varieties, and methods of preparation.

Carbohydrates	Grams
egg	0.50
rice	9.25
beets or	3.00
carrots	2.75
onions	3.75
tomato	7.10
parsley	1.20
celery	1.20
Total	26.58 (approximately)

A One-Pot Rainbow Meal

This is a step-by-step procedure for preparing a Rainbow Meal. We have chosen a variety of colors to make it particularly attractive; however, you can make substitutions from the list of seven food categories. Adjust the cooking time, if necessary. *Remember: Always measure ¼ cup of each ingredient, or the appropriate amount for the individual.* Chicken should be cooked thoroughly. Vegetables should be bright and crunchy.

Equipment needed	Stainless steel pot: 2- or 3-quart size wlth lld
	Stainless steel steamer basket
	Pyrex custard cup
	Cutting board with sharp knife
Complete protein	1 boned chicken thigh
Grain	¼ cup cooked brown rice or millet
Root vegetable	¼ cup raw carrot scrubbed clean, sliced
Red vegetable	Small wedge of red cabbage
Green vegetable	¼ cup broccoli florets
White vegetable	¼ cup cauliflower florets
Leafy green vegetable	Handful spinach leaves
Seasonings	Butter or olive oil, sea salt, or kelp

Place steamer basket and ½ cup of water in pot with lid. Bring water to boil and reduce to medium heat. Place chicken in steamer basket along with rice (in custard cup). Cover pot and steam for approximately 10 to 12 minutes. After 2 minutes, add carrots and cabbage wedge. (Re-cover the pot after each addition.) After 4 additional minutes, add broccoli and cauliflower. Check for doneness. Add spinach leaves for the final minute. Remove all items that are done and, if necessary, steam others, such as the chicken, a few moments longer. Serves 1.

Carbohydrates	Grams
rice	9.25
carrot	4.2
cauliflower	1.5
broccoli	1.5
cabbage	1.75
spinach	1.5
Total	19.7 (approximately)

Rainbow Soup

Allow ¼ cup of each ingredient per person.

Water, 1 cup

Complete protein: lean beef cut into bite-size pieces

Root: carrot, finely chopped

White: onions, minced

Green: celery, sliced

Red: tomato, cut into bite-size pieces

Leafy green vegetable: parsley, snipped

Legumes: cooked lentils

Seasoning: olive oil

Carbohydrates	Grams
lentils	10.0
carrots	2.7
onions	3.4
celery	1.2
tomato	3.0
parsley	1.3
per serving	21.6 approximately

Heat water to boiling and reduce to low heat. Add beef, carrots, and onions, stirring and cooking until softened. Add celery and continue to cook. Add tomato, lentils, and finally parsley. Season as desired, and add ½ to 1 tablespoon of olive oil per person before serving.

This soup can be prepared in large quantity and frozen in individual serving-size containers. It makes an unusual but excellent Rainbow Breakfast.

Rainbow Salad Bar

This makes a beautiful party buffet. Set out an assortment of leafy greens, sliced or chopped vegetables, chilled beans and/or grains, and bite-size cubes of meat, using an individual serving bowl for each item. Prepare grated vegetables just before serving to avoid deterioration. Arrange several different items on a large tray and provide spoons or tongs for servings. Here are some suggestions to stir your imagination:

Leafy greens, torn into bite-size pieces:

> alfalfa sprouts
>
> Chinese cabbage, slivered
>
> lettuce leaves
>
> spinach
>
> watercress

Green vegetables:

> bell pepper, sliced
>
> broccoli florets, raw
>
> celery, sliced
>
> peas, steamed
>
> snap peas, raw
>
> zucchini, raw, sliced

Root vegetables:

> beets, slivered or grated
>
> carrots, slivered or grated
>
> jicama, in cubes or strips
>
> radishes, sliced

White vegetables:

> cauliflower, in florets
>
> corn, freshly picked and raw
>
> cucumber, sliced or chopped

Red vegetables:

> red cabbage, shredded
>
> red pepper (sweet), sliced or chopped
>
> cherry tomatoes, whole
>
> tomatoes, chopped

Beans, cooked and drained:

> chickpeas
>
> kidney beans
>
> lentils

Grains, cooked, chilled, and fluffed with a fork. They should be crumbly:

> millet
>
> rice

Meats or equivalent, cooked and cut into strips or cubes:

> beef
>
> chicken
>
> sliced fish
>
> hard-boiled eggs

Dressings: Offer one or more of the dressings from this book (see pages 148–158) or have olive oil and lemon juice available with little bowls of freshly snipped parsley, chives, other herbs, salt, and kelp in shakers. For non-*Candida* guests, you may wish to add a basket of crackers or warm bread and butter, or a bowl of grated cheese. Just remember, these are *not* in the *Candida* diet.

THE MODIFIED MEAL PLAN

This meal plan is based on a variety of healthful recipes that exclude foods detrimental to the *Candida* patient. There are many other benefits bestowed by this healing diet, in addition to the control of *Candida* infection.

Freshness is the basis for the eating plan, which emphasizes elimination of food additives and mold-contaminated foods as well as fermented beverages and foods. You will discover that you will begin to lose the food addictions that once fed your *Candida*. You will acquire a new taste for healthful, freshly prepared meals.

The recipes selected combine the basic foods of your diet in new and interesting ways. Basic preparation techniques are given for meats, poultry, beans, grains, and egg dishes that retain freshness but retard spoilage.

Candida patients must be especially careful in the selection, storage, and preparation of foods in order to gain full nutritional benefit.

Seasoning for Nutrition and Pleasure

Using herbs and spices is a wonderful way to add flair to a simple meal. Also, many herbs and spices are reported to possess health-giving properties. These include allspice, cinnamon, clove, coriander, dill, garlic, onion, mustard, oregano, rosemary, summer savory, and thyme. Select fresh varieties as much as possible, since dried herbs are mold-prone. The use of fresh herbs may become your trademark as a cook, and the kudos may stimulate you to start growing your own.[8]

You will want to start scissor-snipping your crop. To scissor-snip herbs in a cup, open and close the scissors repeatedly, cutting through the herbs until you have the small size desired. Some varieties may need to be purchased prepackaged at the food stores. Check labels for any additions of sugar, yeast, or additives that you need to avoid.

Use pasteurized butter only if certified raw butter is unavailable. The latter adds valuable nutrients as well as flavor to dishes. Olive oil, too, is nutritious and brings a distinct flavor and aroma to dishes. For a quick dressing, combine freshly-squeezed lemon juice with olive oil.[9] Keep a small quantity in the refrigerator and add scissor-snipped parsley, chives, or mint. It will remain fresh for a few days and add zest to vegetables and salads.

Salt is included in the following recipes (see page 22). You can choose to use it or not, a determination best made in consultation with your physician. If there is no medical problem, it will be your personal choice. Whole Celtic sea salt is preferable to refined salt. An unrefined salt containing trace minerals is also available.

Recipes

Naturopath David Getoff suggests that we think of the surface area of a grain of wheat, oat, corn, and so forth, and compare this to the surface area of a finely ground grain. This immense increase in surface area is one reason that flours have such an impact on our blood sugar. Eating anything made with flour is similar to eating sugar, in terms of its impact on our bodies. Think before you indulge, and then do so most judiciously. Cooked whole grains are the least stressful way to consume grains; for instance, use whole grain wild rice instead of rice flour.

BREAKFAST CEREALS

Psyllium Seed Beverage or Breakfast

Beverage:

   1 heaping teaspoon ground
   psyllium seed

   1 cup water

Pour ground psyllium seeds into glass and stir briskly. Drink at once as a bulk-forming supplement. Follow with another glass of water.

Breakfast:

> 2 heaping teaspoons ground psyllium seed
>
> 1 cup broth, liquid from steamed vegetables, or herb tea

Stir psyllium seed into steaming or cold broth or liquid and serve as cereal. Be sure to follow serving with another 1 cup of liquid.

Cornmeal Mush

> 1 cup boiling water
>
> ½ teaspoon kelp or dulse
>
> ¼ cup freshly ground undegerminated cornmeal
>
> ¼ cup cold water

Carbohydrates	Grams
cornmeal	27.0
per serving	13.5

In top of double boiler, directly on burner, bring 1 cup of water to boil. Add kelp or dulse. Meanwhile, mix cornmeal with ¼ cup cold water. Add this mixture to boiling water, stirring constantly and carefully. (It will bubble.) Continue to cook about 3 minutes. Then return top to double boiler bottom, cover, and continue steaming about 15 minutes, stirring often. Serve with butter. Serves 2.

Cream of Grain Cereal

2 tablespoons any whole grain: rice, wheat, oats, barley, rye

½ cup boiling water

Carbohydrates	Grams
rice	10.0
wheat	8.5
barley	19.0
rye	17.0
oats	11.5

Grind grain in mini-mill. Stir into boiling water. Reduce heat, cover, and simmer 5 minutes. Serve with thick cream, Fake Cream (see page 179) or butter. Serves 1.

Flaxseed Cereal

¼ cup flaxseed, freshly ground in
mini-mill

½ cup boiling water

Slowly stir flaxseed into boiling water. Mix well and cover pot.
Remove from stove and allow to mellow on trivet for about 5
minutes. Serve with thick cream, Fake Cream (see page 179), or
butter. Serves 1.

Oat Bran Cereal

⅓ cup oat bran[10]

1 cup boiling water

Carbohydrates	Grams
per serving	16

Stir oat bran very slowly into the boiling water, stirring
constantly. Return to boil. Reduce heat and cook until desired
thickness, approximately 2 to 3 minutes, stirring often. Remove
from heat and serve with melted butter. Serves 1.

Steamed Whole Grain Cereal

1 cup boiling water

⅛ cup any whole grain: wheat, oats, barley, rye

Carbohydrates	Grams
wheat	11.3
oats	15.2
barley	25.3
rye	22.6

The night before serving, bring 1 cup water to boil. Stir in grain. Return to boil and simmer 10 minutes. Cover and let sit overnight. Next morning bring mixture to simmer, adding more water if necessary. Continue heating until of desired consistency, about 5 minutes for oats, 10 minutes for wheat or barley, and 15 to 30 minutes for rye. Serve with thick cream or butter. Serves 2.

EGGS

Health/natural food stores sell good quality eggs produced by free-range chickens. Try them! The shells should be uniform in shape, smooth, and dense, so you really have to tap sharply on the rim of the skillet in order to crack them. When the raw egg falls onto a plate or dish, it displays a well-rounded yolk of bright orange, surrounded by a clearly defined circle of egg white. You should be able to lift the yolk with your fingers and draw the white of the egg with it.[11]

Soft-cooked Eggs

Use a small saucepan if you are cooking only one or two eggs. Place eggs in saucepan, cover with water. Heat water, using a medium setting, until it begins to boil. Turn off heat, cover pot, and allow the eggs to sit for 5 minutes. Remove eggs from hot water. Rinse them under cold water to stop cooking process.

Hard-cooked Eggs

Initially, plan to cook an extra egg that you can use to check for doneness. You will then have the experience for future reference. Submerge large eggs in sufficient water to cover them. Cook uncovered over medium heat until water bubbles begin to appear. Reduce heat, cover pot, and continue to simmer for 24 minutes. Do not overcook. Open your extra egg under cold water and check yolk for doneness. There should be a hint of bright yellow in the center. If it is cooked sufficiently, use a slotted spoon and immediately remove the remaining eggs from the pot and plunge them into a bowl of cold water. Allow them to remain for 5 minutes, return them to the hot water for 2 minutes, and then remove them. You can now peel them effortlessly under cold water.

Basic Omelet

2 eggs

2 tablespoons water

Dash salt

Seasonings as desired

1 tablespoon butter

Carbohydrates	Grams
eggs	1.0
butter	0.1
Total	1.1

Beat eggs. Add water, salt, and seasonings and beat until blended. Melt butter in skillet over low heat. Pour in egg mixture, and as it cooks, push uncooked portion of egg mixture to outside edge, allowing uncooked egg to reach hot pan surface. Tilt pan as necessary. While top is still slightly moist, roll omelet or fold in half and slide onto plate. Serves 1.

Curried Vegetable Omelet

2 tablespoons butter

¾ cup onions, slivered

2 slices ginger root

1 clove garlic, cut in half

1 teaspoon curry powder

6 tablespoons turkey broth

1 tablespoon butter

3 or 4 eggs

2 tablespoons water

¾ cup bell pepper, cut into thin strips

1¼ cups bok choy leaves, cut into strips

½ cup snow peas

½ cup celery, sliced diagonally

Carbohydrates	Grams
butter	0.3
onions	12.0
curry	1.1
eggs (4)	2.0
bell pepper	2.9
bok choy	2.2
snow peas	5.0
celery	2.5
Total	28.0
per serving	14.0

Over low heat, melt butter in large skillet. Cut onions lengthwise in slivers. Sauté with ginger root and garlic until soft. Discard garlic and ginger. Add curry powder and broth and simmer. Meanwhile, melt butter over low heat in a second skillet. Beat eggs and water and pour into second skillet. Let cook a few minutes. Now add remaining vegetables to onion mixture, cover and simmer. When eggs are done, but still moist, fold in half and serve on plate. Spoon vegetables over eggs. Serves 2.

Variation: Spinach or other greens may be used in place of bok choy.

Spanish Omelet

¼ cup water

¼ cup onions, chopped

¼ cup celery, chopped

¼ cup green pepper, chopped

¼ cup zucchini or crookneck squash, chopped

1 tablespoon arrowroot (optional)

2 tablespoons water

½ cup tomato, chopped

2 eggs

1 teaspoon butter

¼ cup parsley, scissor-snipped

Carbohydrates	Grams
onions	4.0
celery	1.3
green pepper	1.0
zucchini	1.4
arrowroot	7.0
tomato	5.0
eggs	1.0
butter	0.1
parsley	1.2
Total	22.0

Begin cooking onions in water in vapor seal pot over medium heat, reducing heat to low when water begins to boil.[12] (If vapor seal is unavailable, increase water.) Add celery, green pepper, and squash and continue cooking until soft. Do not overcook. Meanwhile, stir arrowroot into water, mixing well. Move vegetables to edge of pan and stir arrowroot mixture into cooking water. Add tomatoes, reduce heat to simmer, and cover. Beat eggs. Melt butter in skillet over low heat. Pour eggs into pan and allow to cook gently. When done, fold omelet and remove from pan. Spoon sauce over omelet. Sprinkle parsley over all, and serve. Serves 1.

Spiced Eggs

The sweet flavor of the nutmeg blends nicely with that of the onions in this recipe.

Carbohydrates	Grams
onions	4.0
squash	2.8
spinach	1.0
eggs (2)	1.0
butter	0.1
tomato	2.5
Total	11.4

¼ cup water

¼ cup onions, sliced

½ cup summer squash, chopped

½ cup each spinach, bok choy, and watercress, torn into small pieces

1 or 2 eggs

⅛ teaspoon nutmeg

1 to 2 teaspoons butter

¼ cup tomato, sliced

Cook onions in a vapor seal pot over low heat. (If vapor seal is unavailable, increase water.) As onions begin to soften, add squash. Cook 4 or 5 minutes. Add leafy greens and cook until soft. Do not overcook. Spoon vegetables into a bowl, reserving cooking water. Beat eggs and add nutmeg and 2 tablespoons cooking water. Melt butter over low heat and pour eggs into pan. Let cook a few minutes. While top is still moist, fill with vegetables. When eggs are done, fold omelet and serve on a plate. Serves 1.

Rainbow Frittata or Kuku

1 tablespoon olive oil, butter, or coconut butter

2 tablespoons yellow bell pepper, finely cut

2 tablespoons zucchini or celery, finely cut

2 tablespoons red bell pepper or tomato, seeded and chopped

2 tablespoons parsley, cilantro, or other greens such as chard, mustard, etc. (you can add up to 1 cup of greens), slivered

2 tablespoons carrot or Jerusalem artichoke, shredded

2 tablespoons onion, shredded

6 eggs (1 per serving) beaten with a whisk

Carbohydrates	Grams
oil or butter	0
yellow bell pepper	0.5
zucchini	0.5
red bell pepper	0.5
parsley	0.5
carrot	1.4
onion	2.0
eggs (6)	3.0
Total	8.4

Place tablespoon olive oil or butter or coconut butter in sauté pan, and add the vegetables. Sauté vegetables several minutes. When soft and golden, pour egg into pan. As it starts to congeal, carefully lift frittata with edge of spatula to allow the egg to run under the mass of frittata. Add more coconut butter if needed. Cover pan and cook over low heat until rest of egg congeals with vegetables.

APPETIZERS

Tortilla Chips

If you wish to slip a few tortilla chips into a bowl of vegetables, try this recipe. Mix the chips with raw carrots, celery, bell peppers, cucumbers, broccoli, cauliflower, turnips, jicama, Jerusalem artichokes, zucchini, or cooked globe artichoke leaves.

Corn tortillas 5" size, commercial

Carbohydrates	Grams
8 chips	5.0

Preheat oven to 400°F. Cut tortilla into 8 pieces. Place on a cookie sheet and bake 6 minutes. Turn and bake 3 more minutes.

NOTE: *Candida* patients should limit themselves to not more than six chips, and should not use chips with bean dips. Instead, try the avocado (page 54), tuna (page 56), eggplant (page 57), or deviled egg (page 51) dips. Also, omit beans and grains from the next meal.

Chicken Liver Pâté

1½ cups chicken livers

¼ cup onions, minced

1 clove garlic, minced

2 tablespoons chicken fat

½ cup concentrated chicken broth

Pinch ground allspice, mace, and thyme

Carbohydrates	Grams
livers	15.0
onions	3.0
garlic	0.5
Total	18.5
¼ cup serving	4.5

Rinse chicken livers and drain on paper towel. Chop coarsely and set aside. Cook onions and garlic in chicken fat over low heat until onions are soft. Add livers. Cook over a low heat for another minute or so, stirring occasionally. Add chicken broth, stir, cover and simmer 7 or 8 minutes longer or until livers are firm and no longer pink. Puree in a blender or mash well with potato masher or fork. Add spices and blend. Chill 2 to 3 hours. Mixture will thicken. Serve as a dip for raw vegetables. Makes about 1 cup.

NOTE: Chicken livers should be from biologically raised poultry; otherwise, they may have a residue of arsenicals or cadmium. If such poultry is unavailable, use calf's or lamb's liver.

Liver Pâté

½ pound leftover broiled lamb
or calf's liver

¼ cup Homemade Mayonnaise
(see page 155)

Herbed salt

1 clove garlic, pressed

1 hard-boiled egg, chopped

1 cup chopped celery, parsley,
and/or other vegetables

Carbohydrates	Grams
liver (½ pound)	9.0
mayonnaise	0.6
garlic	0.5
egg	0.5
vegetables	6.0
Total	16.6

Grind any amount of leftover liver in meat grinder or blender.
Add Homemade Mayonnaise, salt, garlic, egg, and vegetables,
and mix. Serve with yeast-free crackers or raw vegetables. Makes
about 2 cups.

Salmon Pâté

2 cups fresh cooked salmon, drained

⅓ cup Homemade Mayonnaise (see page 155)

3 artichoke hearts, steamed and mashed

1 green onion, chopped

3 tablespoons fresh or
1 teaspoon dried dill weed

¼ teaspoon mustard powder

1 tablespoon lemon juice

Carbohydrates	Grams
salmon	0.0
mayonnaise	0.8
artichoke	2.5
onion	0.8
lemon	1.0
Total	5.1

Remove skin and bones from salmon, and puree in a blender or mash well with a fork. Add remaining ingredients and blend. Chill for 2 to 3 hours. Garnish with cucumber slices and serve with raw vegetables and yeast-free crackers. Makes 2 cups.

Tongue Pâté

1 pound beef or calf's tongue, cooked

2 shallots, 4 or 5 scallions, or 2 tablespoons onions, minced

½ cup celery

2 tablespoons butter

2 tablespoons cooking broth from tongue

½ teaspoon basil, scissor-snipped

1 teaspoon oregano, scissor-snipped

1 stick soft butter

1 teaspoon lemon juice

½ cup parsley, scissor-snipped

Seasoning salt to taste

Carbohydrates	Grams
tongue	2.0
scallions	3.2
celery	2.3
butter	1.0
lemon	0.4
parsley	2.5
Total	11.4

Skin and trim cooked tongue and blend or finely grind it. Sauté vegetables in butter, broth, and herbs. Mix ground mixture, soft butter, lemon juice, and parsley. Mold or shape into pâté and chill one hour. Serve with raw vegetables. Freeze any leftover pâté. Makes about 2 cups.

Deviled Egg Dip

4 hard-cooked eggs, shelled
(see page 40)

4 tablespoons Homemade
Mayonnaise (see page 155)

⅛ teaspoon nutmeg, or to taste
(optional)

½ teaspoon dry mustard
(optional)

Carbohydrates	Grams
eggs	2.0
mayonnaise	0.7
herbs	1.0
Total	3.7

Blend all ingredients. Chill. Serve with raw vegetables. Makes
1 cup.

Variation: Season to taste with other herbs such as curry powder,
tarragon, or basil.

Eggplant Caviar

This mixture, also known as Poor Man's Caviar, can be used as a dip with raw vegetables or to stuff celery.

1½ cups onions, diced

2 cloves garlic, minced

2 tablespoons butter

1 medium eggplant, chopped

⅓ cup water

¼ cup olive oil

¼ cup lemon juice

2 tablespoons fresh basil, minced, or 1 teaspoon dried basil

2 tablespoons sesame seeds (optional)

Carbohydrates	Grams
onions	21.0
garlic	1.0
butter............................	0.2
eggplant......................	18.0
lemon...........................	4.8
sesame seeds	3.3
Total............................	48.3
per ¼ cup	6.0

Soften onion and garlic in butter over low heat. Add eggplant and water. Cover pot and cook over medium heat for 2 minutes. Reduce heat and simmer 10 minutes. Stir in remaining ingredients. Puree in two batches in blender. Chill. Makes approximately 2 cups.

Garbanzo Dip

		Carbohydrates	Grams
2 cups garbanzo beans, cooked and drained (save liquid)		garbanzo beans 122.0	
¼ to ½ cup green onions, chopped		green onions ....4.0 (½ cup)	
2 cloves garlic, minced		garlic 1.8	
2 tablespoons lemon juice		lemon juice....................2.4	
½ cup olive oil		olive oil ....trace	
2 cups parsley, chopped		parsley 10.2	
½ teaspoon dried or 1 tablespoon fresh basil		herbs 0.4	
¼ cup sesame seeds (optional)		sesame seeds 5.3	
		1½ cups 146.1	

Puree all ingredients in blender at low speed. If mixture is too thick, add a little cooking water from beans. Chill. Serve with raw vegetables. Makes 1½ cups.

NOTE: This dip, very high in carbohydrates, should be consumed in limited amounts.

Guacamole Dip

1 cup avocado (1 large)

¼ cup onions, grated or finely chopped

¼ to ½ cup tomato, finely chopped

1 tablespoon lemon juice

1 clove garlic, minced (optional)

¼ cup fresh cilantro leaves, finely chopped

Salt and/or kelp to taste

Carbohydrates	Grams
avocado	15.0
onions	3.8
tomato (½ cup)	5.0
lemon juice	1.2
garlic	0.9
cilantro	0.5
per cup	26.4

Puree all ingredients in electric blender or mash avocado with a fork and mix in other ingredients. Chill. Serve with fresh raw vegetables. Makes 1 cup.

Variation: Substitute sweet basil or other favorite herbs if cilantro is unavailable.

Mexican Bean Dip

1 cup pinto beans, cooked

1 cup tomato, finely chopped

¼ cup (or less) olive oil

½ teaspoon chili powder

½ teaspoon cumin

Salt and/or kelp to taste

Carbohydrates	Grams
pinto beans	60.5
tomato	10.0
olive oil	trace
seasoning	1.0
per cup	71.5
Variations:	
kidney beans	53.0

Puree beans in a ricer (Foley mill) or mash with a fork. Add rest of ingredients and continue to rice or mash. Serve with vegetable as a dip. Makes about 1 cup.

NOTE: *Candida* patients need to limit themselves to a few tablespoons and omit beans and grain at the subsequent meal. This dip can be frozen in small portions and carried along with vegetables (cucumber, celery, and jicama strips, etc.) in a box lunch.

Variations: Add 1 clove garlic, ¼ cup finely minced onion, and some finely minced chili peppers. Substitute kidney beans for pinto beans.

Mock Tuna Dip

This dip may be used to stuff celery or as a dip for fresh raw vegetables.

1 cup fish, cooked and cooled (substitute canned tuna if fresh fish is unavailable)

1 cup celery, finely chopped

1 cup parsley, minced

½ cup green onion, minced

¼ cup bell pepper, minced

¼ cup Homemade Mayonnaise (see page 155)

½ teaspoon dried or
1 tablespoon fresh tarragon, scissor-snipped

½ teaspoon dried or
1 tablespoon fresh dill weed, scissor-snipped

Carbohydrates	Grams
fish	0.0
celery	4.0
parsley	5.0
green onion	3.0
bell pepper	2.4
mayonnaise	0.7
herbs	1.0
Total	16.1

Mash fish and mix with chopped vegetables, mayonnaise, and herbs. Makes 2 cups.

Split Pea-Curry Dip

½ cup dried split peas

1½ cups water

2 tablespoons butter

2 tablespoons onions, chopped

½ cup carrot, sliced

¼ teaspoon curry powder

Carbohydrates	Grams
cooked split peas	42.0
butter	0.2
onions	2.0
carrot	5.5
curry powder	0.9
per cup	50.6

Cook peas until well done, about 1½ hours. If necessary, add more water to prevent burning. Allow excess water to cook off. Cool. (Peas should be the consistency of applesauce.) Sauté onions and carrots in butter over low heat. Stir into split peas. Add curry powder. Blend mixture until carrots are well mashed. Mixture will thicken as it cools. Serve as a dip for raw vegetables. Makes about 1 cup.

Green Garlic Pâté

3 or 4 fresh green garlic bulbs

¼ teaspoon Celtic sea salt

¾ cup extra virgin organic olive oil or ¼ pound of butter (raw is best if you can find it)

Carbohydrates	Grams
3 garlic bulbs (30 cloves)	30
Celtic sea salt	0
olive oil or butter	0
Total	30

Carefully wash fresh garlic and cut-up bulbs, leaves, and roots with salt, and add butter and/or olive oil as you process the pâté in the blender. Use sparingly for great flavor!

SOUPS

Asparagus Soup

1½ cups asparagus stalks

1 cup concentrated chicken broth

2 tablespoons butter

¼ cup shallots or onions, chopped

1 cup celery, chopped

½ cup summer squash, sliced

1½ cups parsley, chopped

½ teaspoon dried or 1 tablespoon fresh basil

Carbohydrates	Grams
asparagus	7.5
broth	1.5
butter	0.2
shallots	6.8
celery	4.7
squash	2.8
parsley	7.5
herbs	0.4
Total	31.4
per serving	15.7

Chop asparagus stalks into 1-inch pieces. Simmer the tough stems in chicken broth for 20 to 30 minutes. In another pan, melt butter over low heat, and add tender asparagus stems, shallots, celery, and summer squash. Sauté until barely soft. Do not overcook. Add parsley and basil to mixture. Discard tough asparagus stems and add chicken broth to mixture. Pour into blender and blend for about a minute. Serves 2.

Avocado-Asparagus Soup

1 pound asparagus, chopped

1 cup water

¼ cup onions, chopped

¼ teaspoon salt (optional)

1 avocado, cut into chunks

2 eggs

Carbohydrates	Grams
asparagus	10.0
onions	4.0
avocado	12.6
eggs	1.0
Total	27.6
per serving	13.8

Simmer asparagus lightly in 1 cup water until just tender. Pour with water into blender, add onion and salt, and puree at low speed. Add avocado and eggs and blend until smooth. Add broth or water to thin if needed. Serve hot or chilled. Serves 2.

Fresh Avocado-Tomato Soup

You can serve this soup warm or chilled.

4 large tomatoes

1 medium avocado

2 green onions

¼ teaspoon ground dill seed

Dash cayenne

1 cup chicken broth

1 teaspoon kelp

Seasoning salt to taste

1 cup parsley, minced

1 cup celery, finely diced

1 tomato, finely chopped

Carbohydrates	Grams
tomato	40.0
avocado	12.6
green onions	2.0
parsley	5.1
celery	5.0
tomato	10.0
seasonings	2.0
Total	76.7
1 of 4 servings	19.2
1 of 3 servings	25.6

Puree all ingredients except last three in blender at low speed. Stir soup mixture into remaining vegetables and warm over low heat, if desired. Or serve cold. Serves 3 to 4.

Hot Borscht

½ cup raw potato with skins, finely diced

½ cup onions, diced

1 cup beets, diced

2 cups cabbage, slivered (Chinese cabbage is acceptable)

¼ cup butter

¾ cup chicken broth

2 tablespoons lemon juice

2 tablespoons parsley or chives, scissor-snipped

Carbohydrates	Grams
potato	12.9
onions	7.5
beets	13.4
cabbage	8.0
butter	0.4
lemon juice	2.5
parsley	0.6
Total	45.3
per serving	22.6

Cook potato over low heat in a small amount of water until soft. Meanwhile, cook remaining vegetables over low heat in butter with a small amount of water until soft. When potatoes are cooked, add chicken broth and simmer until warmed. Puree this mixture at low speed in blender. Add potato puree and lemon juice to vegetable mixture, reheat, and serve. Garnish with snipped herbs. Serves 2.

NOTE: *Candida* patients should limit themselves to 1 serving of this soup and omit beans and grains from the same meal.

Chicken Soup

	Carbohydrates	Grams
1 chicken, cut up	chicken	0
2 quarts water or broth	celery	9.4
4 cloves garlic, sliced (optional, to taste)	carrots	22.0
	onions	30.0
2 cups each celery, carrots, onions, peas, sliced	peas	38.0
	garlic	3.6
½ cup cooked brown rice	rice	18.5
½ cup chopped parsley	parsley	2.5
Herbs and seasoning to taste	Total	124.0
	per serving	12.4

Simmer chicken in water or stock for 40 minutes. Add vegetables and rice and simmer for 20 additional minutes. Serve broth and vegetables with chicken meat and top with scissor-snipped fresh parsley. Add herbs according to taste. Serves 10.

NOTE: Freeze surplus soup in portion-size containers. It is useful to have on hand some frozen portions of clear broth.

Variation: ¼ cup raw rice may be added to the water and simmered with the chicken.

Chicken Soup II

3 pounds chicken backs, necks, and wings

3 quarts water

3 carrots, sliced

4 stalks celery, sliced

4 cloves garlic, chopped

½ bunch parsley, chopped

4 green onions or 1 medium onion, chopped

1 teaspoon dried thyme (optional)

Carbohydrates	Grams
chicken	0.0
carrots	7.0
celery	5.0
garlic	2.0
parsley	1.0
onions	4.0
Total	19.0
per 1 cup	1.5

Bring chicken and water to boil. Reduce heat and simmer, covered, for 1 hour. Add vegetables and thyme and simmer 15 additional minutes or until tender. Makes 12 cups.

NOTE: Freeze surplus soup.

Mexican Chicken Soup

1 quart chicken broth

1 cup onions, chopped

1 cup celery, chopped

1½ cups cooked chicken, slivered

¾ cup brown rice, cooked

1 cup cabbage, finely shredded

1 cup tomatoes, diced

¼ cup radishes

¼ cup scallions, chopped

1 cup parsley, chopped

½ cup green pepper, chopped

¾ cup avocado, cubed (optional)

½ cup fresh cilantro leaves

Salt and/or kelp to taste

Carbohydrates	Grams
chicken broth	6.0
onions	13.7
celery	4.7
rice	28.6
cabbage	6.0
tomatoes	10.3
radishes	2.0
scallions	1.6
parsley	5.0
green pepper	2.5
avocado	9.2
cilantro	1.0
Total	90.6
1 of 3 servings	30.2
1 of 4 servings	22.7

Bring chicken broth to a boil and reduce heat to simmer. Add onions and celery, and simmer a few minutes; add chicken and rice. As broth simmers, add remaining ingredients and continue stirring and simmering for 3 to 4 minutes longer, until vegetables are piping hot but still crunchy. Serves 3 to 4.

Variations: If cilantro is unavailable, substitute ½ teaspoon thyme or 1 tablespoon fresh thyme. You can place the raw vegetables on a platter and invite guests to transfer their choices to individual soup bowls. Then ladle the hot broth over the raw vegetables for a steaming and crunchy soup.

Egg Drop Soup

2 cups chicken broth

1 scallion, sliced

1 egg

Carbohydrates	Grams
broth	3.0
scallion	2.0
egg	0.5
Total	5.5
per serving	2.8

Warm scallion gently in broth. Beat egg and dribble it into hot soup while stirring rapidly so that egg coagulates into thin noodlelike strands. Continue to stir and cook only until egg is firm. Serves 2.

Garden Soup

A light soup, good any time. The colorful vegetables nourish the soul as well as the body.

1½ cups water

¼ cup purple-topped turnip, chopped

½ cup green beans, chopped

½ cup carrots, sliced

½ cup zucchini or summer squash, sliced

½ cup Chinese cabbage, shredded

1½ cups parsley, chopped

½ cup tomato, chopped

Generous pinch thyme, rosemary, marjoram

Dash seasoning salt (optional)

Carbohydrates	Grams
turnip	2.0
green beans	4.0
carrots	5.5
squash	3.5
cabbage	1.2
parsley	7.7
tomato	5.0
Total	28.9
per serving	14.4

Bring water to a boil. Add turnip, beans, and carrots. Simmer 3 to 5 minutes. Meanwhile, prepare zucchini and cabbage, and add them to pot. Continue to simmer a few more minutes. Chop parsley and tomato, add and continue to simmer 2 more minutes. Crumble herbs and add them to pot. Add salt if desired. Remove from heat and let sit a minute. Serves 2 generously.

Gazpacho

2 cups tomatoes

¾ cup cucumber

¼ cup green pepper

¾ cup celery with leaves

¼ cup parsley

¼ cup scallions

1 clove garlic

¼ cup lemon or lime juice

1 to 2 tablespoons olive oil

½ teaspoon dried or
1 tablespoon fresh basil

¼ cup chicken broth and/or
¾ cup processed tomato juice
(without additives)

Carbohydrates	Grams
tomatoes	20.0
cucumber	4.0
green pepper	1.0
celery	0.7
parsley	1.3
scallions	2.0
garlic	0.9
lemon juice	4.8
olive oil	0.0
herbs	0.5
tomato juice	8.0
Total	43.2
1 of 4 servings	10.8
1 of 3 servings	14.4

Chop vegetables and put half in blender along with garlic, lemon or lime juice, olive oil, basil, broth, and tomato juice. Puree briefly. Pour into large bowl. Chop remaining vegetables very fine and stir them into blender mixture. Chill and serve. Serves 3 to 4.

Variation: Substitute other herbs, chilies, or chili powder for basil. For a different flavor, stir in ¾ cup steamed, chilled, cubed fish and ¾ cup cooked, chilled rice. Add more herbs if desired.

Hearty Lentil Soup

½ cup lentils

2 cups water

1 onion, chopped

3 stalks celery, chopped

1 carrot, chopped

3 tomatoes, chopped

1 clove garlic, minced

½ cup parsley, chopped

2 tablespoons tomato paste

2 tablespoons fresh or
1 teaspoon dried thyme

Salt to taste

2 tablespoons olive oil

Carbohydrates	Grams
lentils	40.0
onion	15.0
celery	6.0
carrot	7.0
tomato	22.0
garlic	0.9
parsley	2.6
tomato paste	6.0
herbs	1.0
olive oil	0.0
Total	100.5
per serving	25.1

Bring lentils to a boil, reduce heat and simmer for about 1 hour.
(If you are using sprouted lentils, heat water only to near boil,
reduce heat, and simmer lentils 5 to 10 minutes.) Add chopped
onions, celery, and carrots and stir while simmering 10 additional
minutes. Add chopped tomatoes and minced garlic and simmer
3 more minutes. Add chopped parsley, tomato paste, thyme, and
salt if desired. Simmer 3 more minutes. Stir in olive oil and serve.
(Consistency may be thick. Add water if you desire to thin it.)
Serves 4.

Variations: This recipe, adapted from a conventional one, has less starch (lentils and carrots) and more non-starchy vegetables (onion and celery). To reduce the carbohydrate content, use fewer lentils and omit the tomato paste. Serve this soup with a green salad or leafy green vegetables for balance of vegetables.

NOTE: The *Candida* patient should limit this soup to 1 serving.

Marrow Soup

Have your butcher split or slice shank or knuckle bones with an electric saw. Short ribs, oxtail, lamb trimmings, or other inexpensive cuts of boned meat are good, too. Reserve the bones.

Allow 2 cups of water for every cup of lean meat and bone. Cover the bones with pure cold water and let stand 1 hour. Heat gently to 175°F, and cook for 12 hours or until meat falls off the bone. Cool uncovered, and then remove the bones. Refrigerate. Do not skim off the fat until ready to reheat.

To use: Gently simmer the meat and any fresh vegetables briefly in some of the broth until the vegetables are tender. Freeze surplus marrow soup in single portion-size containers.

Carbohydrates	Grams
.................................0	

Minestrone Soup

A colorful winter warmer-upper.

¾ cup cooked beans (white, kidney, or limas or fresh peas)

2 tablespoons butter

½ cup onions, chopped

1 clove garlic, minced

3 cups broth

1 cup carrots, sliced

½ cup green beans, chopped

½ cup zucchini, cut in half lengthwise and then sliced

¾ cup celery tops, sliced

2 cups green cabbage or Swiss chard, slivered

½ teaspoon dried oregano

½ teaspoon dried thyme

1 cup parsley, chopped

1 cup tomato, chopped

½ teaspoon salt or kelp

2 tablespoons olive oil (optional)

Carbohydrates	Grams
beans	30.0
butter	0.2
onions	7.0
garlic	0.5
carrots	16.7
green beans	4.0
zucchini	4.0
celery	3.0
cabbage	12.0
parsley	5.0
tomato	12.0
herbs, oil	0.0
Total	94.4
per serving	23.6

Cook beans (see page 78) and set aside. Sauté onions and garlic in butter until soft. Add broth and bring to a boil over medium heat. Add carrots and green beans. Reduce heat and simmer 2 or 3 minutes. Add zucchini and celery and simmer until zucchini begins to soften. Add cabbage and herbs and simmer until cabbage begins to soften. Add beans and allow to warm. Add parsley, tomato, and salt and let simmer another 2 minutes. Add olive oil and serve. Serves 4.

Variation: Add beef, lamb, turkey, or chicken to this soup to make a complete meal. In this case, the broth should match the flavor of the chosen meat.

Soup Salad

We hear that this soup was prescribed by a nutritionally oriented doctor who encouraged his patients to drink it daily.

½ cup water or seasoned broth

1 zucchini with skin, chopped

2 stalks celery with leaves, chopped

½ onion, chopped

6 string beans, finely chopped

½ cup parsley, chopped

1 clove garlic, minced

1 bay leaf

½ teaspoon dried basil

2 tablespoons lemon juice

Salt and/or kelp

Carbohydrates	Grams
zucchini	2.5
celery	4.0
onion	7.5
string beans	3.5
parsley	2.5
garlic	0.9
herbs	0.5
lemon juice	2.4
Total	23.8
per serving	11.9

Bring water to a boil and add vegetables and bay leaf. Reduce heat, cover, and simmer 8 to 10 minutes. Stir in remaining ingredients and cool a few minutes. Remove bay leaf and puree soup in blender. Serves 2.

Tomato-Eggplant Soup

This soup can be served warm or chilled.

¾ cup onions, diced

1 clove garlic, minced

1 tablespoon butter

½ medium eggplant, chopped

3 tablespoons water

1 cup parsley, chopped

1½ cups tomato, chopped

1 tablespoon fresh basil, minced,
or ½ teaspoon dried basil

1½ tablespoons olive oil, or to
taste

2 tablespoons lemon juice

Carbohydrates	Grams
onions	12.0
garlic	0.9
butter	0.1
eggplant	9.2
parsley	5.1
tomato	15.0
herbs	0.4
oil	0.0
lemon juice	2.4
Total	45.1
per serving	22.5

Soften onion and garlic in butter by cooking over low heat. Add
eggplant and water, cover pot, and simmer 10 minutes. Blend
parsley, tomato, basil, oil, and lemon juice in blender. Add the
cooked mixture, puree, and serve. Serves 2.

Tomato-Watercress Soup

1 tablespoon chicken fat or
butter

½ cup leeks, finely chopped

1 garlic clove, minced

1½ cups chicken broth

½ cup potato, cubed

1½ cups tomato, chopped

2 cups watercress leaves,
chopped

½ cup parsley, minced

Carbohydrates	Grams
butter	0.1
leeks	5.5
garlic	0.5
broth	2.3
potato	12.5
tomato	15.0
watercress	4.4
parsley	2.5
Total	42.8
per serving	21.4

Spoon fat into saucepan, add leeks and garlic, and cook covered over low heat for 6 to 8 minutes until tender. Stir occasionally. Add broth and potato. Bring to a boil over medium heat, then reduce heat and simmer until potato is tender, 10 to 15 minutes. Add tomato, watercress, and parsley, and simmer 1 to 2 minutes. Cool to room temperature or chill. Serves 2.

Variations: Substitute zucchini for potato and cook 5 minutes in broth. Substitute onion or scallion for leeks. Substitute cucumber for potato, and add with tomato rather than cooking it.

Quick Vegetable-Beef Soup

Use a chuck roast, cutting meat into bite-size pieces and refrigerating while you simmer the bones with the following ingredients.

2 cups water

2 cups sliced carrots

2 cups sliced onions

2 cups chopped celery

2 cups green beans,
cut into pieces

2 cups chopped cabbage

2 cups chopped fresh tomatoes

Salt to taste

Fresh herbs to taste

Carbohydrates	Grams
chuck roast	0.0
carrots	22.0
onions	20.0
celery	9.4
green beans	16.0
cabbage	12.0
tomatoes	20.0
6 cups	99.4
per serving	16.5

Simmer the first five ingredients, covered, for 20 minutes. Then add the cabbage and meat. Simmer 10 minutes and remove bones. Simmer until meat is tender and then add the chopped fresh tomatoes, seasoned to taste with fresh herbs and sea salt. Simmer 5 minutes. If you can find canned tomatoes or tomato puree without additives and no citric acid, it makes a delightful flavor variation. Be sure to make enough extra to freeze in 1- or 2-cup packages so that it will be ready to thaw and heat when you are famished and need a quick meal. Serves 6.

Vichyssoise

A cold soup for hot weather.

½ cup raw potato, finely diced

¾ cup leeks, thinly sliced

¼ cup onions, finely diced

½ cup celery, finely diced

1 tablespoon butter

½ cup chicken broth (or more, if desired)

½ cup cucumber, finely chopped

½ cup parsley, chopped

½ cup watercress, chopped

1 teaspoon lemon juice (optional)

⅛ teaspoon ground mace

Carbohydrates	Grams
potato	12.9
leeks	8.2
onions	3.5
celery	2.5
butter	0.1
broth	0.8
cucumber	1.8
parsley	2.6
watercress	0.5
lemon juice	0.4
Total	33.3
per serving	16.7

Cook potato in a small amount of water over low heat until soft, and set aside. Sauté leeks, onions, and celery in butter over low heat for a few minutes. Add chicken broth and cook for 10 minutes or until vegetables are soft but not overcooked. Add remaining ingredients to soup. Pour potatoes and their cooking water into blender, add ¾ of soup mixture and puree at low speed. Pour mixture back into soup pan, stir in remaining ¼ of soup and chill. Serves 2.

NOTE: *Candida* patients must limit themselves to 1 serving.

Quick Zucchini Soup

2 cups unpeeled zucchini, coarsely chopped

¼ cup onions, finely chopped

1 cup chicken broth

2 tablespoons butter (optional)

1 cup parsley, chopped

⅛ teaspoon nutmeg

Carbohydrates	Grams
zucchini	11.0
onions	4.0
broth	1.5
butter	0.2
parsley	5.1
nutmeg	0.3
Total	22.1
per serving	11.0

Cook zucchini and onions in chicken broth over low heat until tender. Add butter, parsley, and nutmeg. Let soup cool 2 or 3 minutes, then puree in blender on low speed. Serves 2.

LEGUMES AND GRAINS

Adelle Davis suggests that you presoak dried beans for several hours and then freeze them in the soaking liquid so that cooking time can be cut in half.[13] Simply soak beans for 2 hours in water to cover. Freeze 2 hours, and then cook in a cup of broth or steamed water.

Although peanuts are a member of the legume family, they should be avoided when on a healing diet.[14]

If possible, grind your own grains and use at once. Try to use them sparingly because they are high in carbohydrates. For this reason, use only small amounts of yeast-free breads and crackers and tortillas. Avoid packaged breakfast cereals.

Add cooked grains to soups or salads as crouton substitutes. They soak up the tangy flavor of salad dressing. Store grains in containers with tight-fitting covers to prevent moisture and insect infestation. Place in a cool, dry area to retard rancidity.

Basic Bean Recipe

1 cup dried beans (except lentils or split peas)

1 or 2 bay leaves (helps digestion)

3 cups water

Salt to taste

Carbohydrates	Grams
Most beans are about 40 grams per cup cooked or 10 grams per ¼-cup portion.	

Soak beans in cold water for 6 to 8 hours (in refrigerator if kitchen is warm). Remove any beans that float. Bring beans to a boil and simmer for 1½ to 2½ hours or until tender. Do not add salt until tender. Remove bay leaves.

Quick soak method: Bring water to a boil. Add beans slowly so that boiling does not stop. Remove pot from heat and let stand covered, 1 hour. Cook beans as directed above.

NOTE: Garbanzo beans require more cooking water and cooking time. Use 4 cups of water and cook for 3 hours. Soybeans require 3 hours or more. Lentils and split peas may be cooked, unsoaked, in 3 cups water, for 45 to 60 minutes, or until tender.

Basic Brown Rice

½ cup raw brown rice

1 cup water or weak broth

Carbohydrates	Grams
¼ cup cooked rice	9.3

Rinse and drain rice. Bring water or broth to a boil. Add rice, cover, and allow to simmer for 45 minutes or until fluffy. (Pot should have a tight-fitting lid.) If after 45 minutes the rice still seems tough, add additional boiling water, cover, and continue cooking. Do not stir. Yield: 1¼ cups.

NOTE: *Candida* patients should limit themselves to ¼ cup per meal of any cooked whole grain.

Green Rice

This is an attractive way to serve rice on a hot summer day.

1 cup (packed) parsley or watercress (or ¾ cup parsley and ¼ cup watercress)

¼ cup cilantro or dill weed or fennel

2 tablespoons green onion

1 cup brown rice, cooked and chilled

1 tablespoon olive oil

1 tablespoon lemon juice

Carbohydrates	Grams
parsley	5.1
herbs	1.0
green onion	1.0
rice	37.0
olive oil	0.0
lemon juice	1.2
Total	45.3
per serving	11.3

Run greens through food processor or mince finely with a sharp knife. Mix with rice. Pour olive oil and lemon juice over mixture and stir. Serves 4. Limit yourself to 1 serving.

Kasha (Buckwheat Groats)

2 tablespoons butter

½ cup buckwheat groats

1 cup water

Carbohydrates	Grams
¼ cup serving	8.0

Melt butter and stir in buckwheat groats. Bring water to boil and pour over groats. Simmer 15 minutes. Serves 5.

Variation: Add ¼ cup onions to melted butter.

Lentil Delight

¼ cup butter

½ cup onions, diced

1 cup lentil sprouts or 1 cup
lentils measured after soaking
overnight

½ cup celery, diced

½ cup bell pepper, diced

Carbohydrates	Grams
butter	0.4
onions	7.5
lentils	about 40.0
celery	2.5
bell pepper	1.9
Total	52.3
per serving	13.1

Melt butter over low heat in a heavy pan. Add onions and stir.
Add lentils, celery, and peppers, and cover with a tight lid.
Simmer until lentils are fork-tender. Serves 4.

Millet

	Carbohydrates	Grams
2 cups water		
⅔ cup millet	¼ cup cooked millet	14

Bring water to a boil and stir in millet. Cover pot and simmer 20 to 30 minutes. Millet should be fluffy. Yield: approximately 2 cups.

Homemade Potassium Baking Powder

	Carbohydrates	Grams
1 cup arrowroot flour		
1 cup cream of tartar	1 tablespoon	7
½ cup potassium bicarbonate (purchase from pharmacy)	1 teaspoon	approx. 2

Sift ingredients together and store in a tightly closed jar. Sift again before using and use in the same proportions as commercial baking powder.

Millet Muffins

1 cup freshly ground millet flour
(grind ¼ cup millet at a time
either in a blender or in a
mini-mill)

1 cup carrots, finely grated

1 teaspoon kelp powder

2 tablespoons butter

1 teaspoon potassium baking
powder (see page 83)

¾ cup boiling water

3 eggs, separated

2 tablespoons water

¼ teaspoon maple extract

Carbohydrates	Grams
millet	170.0
carrots	11.0
kelp	1.8
butter	0.2
baking powder	2.0
eggs	1.5
Total	186.5
per muffin	15.5

Preheat over to 375°F. Mix flour, carrots, kelp, butter, and baking
powder. Pour the boiling water over this mixture and stir.
Separate eggs. Add water to the beaten egg yolks and add this to
the flour mixture. Fold in the stiffly beaten egg whites and maple
extract. Fill well-buttered muffin tins ¾ full. Bake for 25 minutes
or until golden brown. Makes 1 dozen muffins.

Oat Bran Crackers

¼ cup boiling water

2 teaspoons butter

½ cup oat bran

Salt to taste

Carbohydrates	Grams
butter	0.1
oat bran	24.0
each cracker	12.0

Preheat over to 350°F. Pour boiling water over butter and oat bran. Add salt and mix well with a fork. Shape dough into two balls, and press each into a round flat cracker with your palms and lay them on a greased cookie sheet. Bake 20 to 25 minutes, or until light brown. Serve hot with a pat of butter. Yield: 2 crackers 3½ inches in diameter.

Oat Bran-Sweet Potato Muffins

2½ cups raw sweet potato, grated

2½ cups oat bran

1 tablespoon baking powder
(see page 83)

1 teaspoon cinnamon

¼ teaspoon allspice

1 cup water

3 eggs, separated

2 tablespoons melted butter

Carbohydrates	Grams
sweet potato	70.0
oat bran	12.0
spices	1.0
eggs	1.5
butter	0.2
12 muffins	192.7
each muffin approximately	16

Preheat over to 400°F. Scrub, peel, and grate the sweet potato or put through food processor. Grate enough to fill 2½ cups. Place sweet potato in mixing bowl and add oat bran. Add baking powder, cinnamon, and allspice. Mix well. Make a depression in the center of this mixture and add water, egg yolks, and melted butter. Beat egg whites and fold into batter. Fill 12 greased muffin cups. Bake for 20 to 25 minutes or until a toothpick inserted into the muffin comes out clean. Freeze the leftover muffins at once. One muffin per meal for *Candida* patients.

Sweet Potato-Oat Bran Pancakes

1 egg

1 medium size sweet potato, peeled, scrubbed, and cubed

2 tablespoons oat bran

¼ teaspoon potassium baking powder (see page 83)

2 tablespoons butter

Carbohydrates	Grams
egg	0.4
sweet potato	33.0
oat bran	6.0
baking powder	0.5
butter	0.2
Total	40.0
each	10.0

Place egg in blender and turn to low speed. Gradually add small amounts of sweet potato. Continue blending, and add the oat bran and baking powder. When mixture is smooth and thick, spoon into melted butter in skillet and sauté until lightly browned on each side. Top with additional butter and serve. Makes 4 pancakes.

Potato Pancakes

1 egg

2 small potatoes, scrubbed and cubed

1 slice onion

2 or more parsley sprigs

2 tablespoons oat bran

⅛ tablespoon potassium baking powder (see page 83)

2 tablespoons butter

Carbohydrates	Grams
egg	approx 0.4
potatoes	34.2
onion	0.8
parsley	0.4
oat bran	6.0
baking powder	0.0
butter	0.2
Total	42.0
per serving	14 or 21

Blend egg, potatoes, onion, and parsley on low speed until finely chopped. Add oat bran and baking powder. Blend on slow speed until well mixed. Melt butter in skillet until just golden. Do not let it turn brown. Sauté by dropping a serving-spoon-size pancake into the melted butter and cooking until golden brown on each side. Serves 2 or 3.

Waffles

3 eggs, separated

⅓ cup water

1½ teaspoons vanilla

1 cup arrowroot flour or oat bran or rice flour or mixture of flour, bran, and polishings from rice

Carbohydrates	Grams
eggs	1.2
vanilla	0.0
arrowroot (1)	112.0
oat bran (2)	48.0
rice flour (3)	85.0
Total	
(1)	113.2
(2)	49.2
(3)	86.2
per waffle	
(1)	28.3
(2)	12.3
(3)	21.5

Separate the eggs. Pour the yolks into the blender. Add water and the vanilla to the yolks. Spoon in flour and blend until smooth. Beat egg whites until stiff. Fold the blended mixture into the egg whites until lightly mixed. Spoon into waffle iron and bake until brown. Serve with butter. Eat only one waffle, and consider it as a bread or toast substitute, minus any sweeteners. Makes 4 waffles.

MEATS AND POULTRY

In addition to a wide assortment of fresh vegetables, a variety of meats, poultry, and seafood is included in your modified diet plan.

Pork is omitted since many nutritionists advise against it, especially for a therapeutic diet.

In addition to starving the *Candida* in your body, you need to rebuild damaged tissue as rapidly as possible. Overcooking meat damages the protein value of the food, makes it less usable, and also renders fat indigestible. For specific and comprehensive cooking instructions on meat preparation, there are several excellent books, including Adelle Davis's *Let's Cook It Right*.[15] This has explicit instructions for a method of "slow cooking" meats and poultry, with charts for cooking times and temperatures for different cuts of meats. Another good book is the *Natural Foods Primer*[16] by Beatrice Trum Hunter, which provides handy tips on proper storing and freezing of meats to ensure retention of valuable nutrients. You may also refer to James Beard's *Theory and Practice of Good Cooking*,[17] Beard's *Fish Cookery*,[18] and Irma S. Rombauer and Marion Rombauer Becker's *Joy of Cooking*[19] for comprehensive food preparation and advice.

Dos and Don'ts

Variety meats such as kidney, heart, and tongue are recommended on a healing diet because they contain exceptional nutrient qualities. However, they spoil quickly and must be used when fresh. Slow cooking is best.

Try to buy poultry that is raised locally and is free of preservatives. Use only freshly purchased meats. Ground meat is more likely to contain mold contaminants, and even after cooking some harmful microorganisms are not destroyed. We wish to emphasize the importance of choosing animal proteins that have not been treated with hormones, antibiotics, or growth stimulants, which may be conveyed to the consumer of these proteins. If possible, choose organically reared and ranged animals, including searching for free-range organic chickens and their eggs.

Barbecuing and frying are very popular cooking methods, but should be avoided. When meat is barbecued, the smoke produced from the fats splattering on the meat from the hot coals is carcinogenic. Nor are fried foods advisable for *Candida* patients.[20] Dried, pickled, and smoked foods are also inadvisable, as they are more likely to have molds. Lightly salting meat at the table is acceptable.

Equipment

A nested set of stainless steel measuring cups and spoons is necessary for the Rainbow portions. Try the ⅛-cup scoop for smaller portions. (This is the size used for ground coffee.)

A meat thermometer is essential for cooking meats properly. It should be inserted into the meat, away from the bone, to determine the internal temperature of the meat as it cooks.

A Crock-Pot is useful for long, slow cooking. Soups or stews can cook for hours at low temperatures, making it possible, if you are away all day, to have the dish completely cooked when you come home.

Stainless steel cooking utensils and one or more stainless steel steamer baskets are recommended to prepare a variety of vegetables for each meal. The pot with a snug cover or vapor seal lid will conduct heat evenly.

An electric blender helps prepare sauces and dressings.

Several sharp knives are essential to cut vegetables, trim fat, and test meat for doneness.

A small toaster/broiler oven is handy to bake chicken, fish, steaks, and chops. Some of these ovens cook more rapidly than conventional ones. In any method used to prepare meat, *don't overcook!* If you cook frozen meat, plan to thaw the day of cooking by setting it out in the refrigerator overnight for the next day.

When broiling steaks, place a 1-inch steak approximately 2 inches from the heat source for 3 to 4 minutes per side for medium rare. If using thicker cuts, cook to an internal temperature of 130° to 135°F.

Broil a 1-inch lamb chop 2 inches from the heat source for 3 to 4 minutes per side for medium rare. The juices should run pink, as all meats continue to cook for several minutes after broiling or roasting.

Broil chicken bone side up first, 4 inches from the heat source for approximately 14 minutes per side. When the juices run clear the chicken should be ready to eat. Of course, the thickness and boniness of a chicken may alter the cooking time slightly.

An old French proverb states, "Cooks are made, roasters are born." Roast your meat at a low temperature (300° to 325°F) throughout the cooking process. Check its internal temperature with a meat thermometer to determine doneness. The temperatures below are for rare meat. Remember, meats continue to cook for 10 to 15 minutes after they are removed from the oven.

Beef	125°F to 130°F	Place thermometer in center cut of chop or steak.
Lamb	130°F to 135°F	
Chicken	160°F to 165°F	
Turkey (unstuffed)	170°F to 175°F	Place thermometer in thickest part of thigh for poultry, but not next to the bone.

Broiled Chicken

1 chicken, quartered

¼ cup lemon juice

¼ cup olive oil

1 clove garlic, crushed

1-inch piece fresh ginger, grated

Carbohydrates	Grams
.........................negligible	

Rinse chicken and pat dry with paper towels. Marinate in lemon juice, oil, garlic, and ginger for 1 to 3 hours in refrigerator. Turn oven to broil. Brush chicken with marinade. Place on baking sheet, cut side up. Broil quickly, about 10 minutes. Turn with tongs and place skin side up. Baste again and bake about 20 minutes at 450°F.

Roast Turkey

12 to 14 pound turkey
(free of additives)

Juice of 1 or 2 lemons

2 celery stalks

2 onion slices

¼ pound or more butter, melted

Salt to taste

Carbohydrates	Grams
.........................negligible	

Preheat oven to 325°F. Rinse turkey gently and pat dry with paper towels. Remove liver, heart, and gizzard from cavity and steam with the neck, a stalk of celery, and slice of onion. (Broth may be added to gravy or frozen for soup.) Remove all fat from cavity and render over low heat while preparing the bird as follows.

Rub the interior cavity with lemon juice. Place a stalk of celery and slice of onion in the cavity. Truss the turkey with twine to close the cavity securely. In a 2-cup measuring cup, pour rendered fat and enough melted butter to make 1 cup. To this mixture add 4 teaspoons of broth from the organ meat and salt to taste. Coat one side of the bird with half of the butter mixture and place it, buttered side up, on a rack in a shallow roasting pan. Roast 1 hour. With hands protected by mitts, turn the turkey to the other side and coat with remaining butter mixture. Roast for 1 hour more. Turn breast side up and baste with juice. Roast for another 25 minutes. Test for doneness by placing thermometer in the thickest part of the thigh (it should register 170° to 175°F) or by testing the legs to see if they move easily.

If you have used a fresh turkey and have a generous amount left over, you may choose to strip it from the bones and make broth from the carcass. Then freeze the leftover turkey in broth in individual serving-size packages that can be reheated quickly. Later you can use the defrosted turkey and broth in "Leftover Turkey Curry" (pages 97–98) or stir-fry recipes.

Turkey Gravy

Dissolve 1 tablespoon arrowroot in ¼ cup cooked broth. Add 2 cups of turkey juices. Heat until arrowroot thickens and clears. Add seasonings and a bit of chopped onion for flavor. Makes 2 cups.

Carbohydrates	Grams
per 2 cups	8.0
per ¼ cup	1.0

Stovetop Holiday Dressing

2 tablespoons turkey fat or butter

1 cup onions, chopped

2 cups celery, chopped (include leaves)

1 cup carrots, chopped

2 cups zucchini, chopped

1 cup rice, cooked (in broth, if possible)

Giblets, cooked and chopped

½ teaspoon dried or
1 tablespoon fresh sage

½ teaspoon dried or
1 tablespoon fresh thyme

Salt and/or kelp to taste

Carbohydrates	Grams
butter............................	0.2
onion	15.0
celery	10.0
carrots	11.0
zucchini	12.4
brown rice	37.0
giblets	3.0
herbs	0.6
Total	89.2
per serving	22.3

Soften onions in fat over low heat. Add celery, carrots, and zucchini and simmer until softened. Add rice, giblets, and seasonings. Allow to warm. Serves 4.

To balance meal: Serve with turkey and lots of other vegetables. It is recommended that you not stuff turkey with dressing.

NOTE: *Candida* patients must limit themselves to 1 serving of dressing and are advised to skip potatoes at this meal—even at Thanksgiving dinner!

Turkey Hash

1 tablespoon butter

½ cup onions, chopped

½ cup potato, chopped

¾ cup celery, sliced

½ cup bell pepper, chopped

¼ cup carrots, sliced

¾ cup cooked turkey, cubed

Broth (optional)

½ cup parsley, finely chopped

Salt and/or kelp to taste

Cayenne pepper or paprika (optional)

Carbohydrates	Grams
butter	0.2
onions	7.5
potato	12.8
celery	5.0
bell pepper	1.9
carrots	3.0
turkey	0.0
parsley	2.5
Total	33.0
per serving	16.5

Melt butter over low heat. Sauté onions and potatoes. When soft, stir in the remaining vegetables (except parsley), turkey, and broth if desired, and cook gently until just slightly crisp. Add parsley and seasoning. Serves 2.

Variations: This recipe calls for leftover frozen turkey, but you can also use other leftover meat, chicken, fish, or fresh meats. However, fresh meats should be added before potato is finished cooking.

NOTE: *Candida* patients should omit beans and grains when eating potatoes.

Leftover Turkey Curry (Mock Stir-Fry)

This is a good way to use leftover turkey that you have frozen in small packages.

2 tablespoons butter

¾ cup onions, slivered

2 slices ginger root

1 clove garlic, cut in half

1 teaspoon curry powder

6 tablespoons turkey broth

¾ cup bell pepper, slivered

½ cup cooked rice (optional)

¾ cup leftover turkey, torn into bite-size pieces

1 cup bok choy leaves, cut into strips

¾ cup snow peas

¾ cup jicama or water chestnuts, cut into strips

Carbohydrates	Grams
butter	0.2
onions	10.0
ginger	0.8
garlic	0.4
curry	1.0
broth	0.0
bell pepper	2.5
rice	18.5
turkey	0.0
bok choy	7.0
peas	8.0
jicama	19.2
with rice	67.2
without rice	49.1
per serving:	
with rice	33.8
without rice	24.5

Melt butter in large skillet over low heat. Cut onion in quarters the long way, and cut slivers from the quarters. Sauté onion, ginger root, and garlic. Remove garlic and ginger. Add curry powder, broth, and bell pepper strips. When broth has warmed, add rice, turkey pieces, and bok choy and cover pan. When bok choy has wilted, add snow peas and jicama and warm for a minute or so. Serves 2 generously.

NOTE: This method is preferable to stir-frying. Except for the onion, these vegetables are being warmed rather than cooked to retain their nutrients.

Broiled Butterflied Lamb Leg

Several cloves garlic

Rosemary

Marjoram

2 tablespoons butter

1 leg of lamb (ask the butcher to butterfly the lamb to lie flat like steak)

Carbohydrates	Grams
.........................negligible	

Cream seasoning in butter and spread on non-fat side of meat. Broil about 5 inches from heat for 15 minutes per side. The lamb should be pink inside, not brown or gray, when done. Slice and serve as you would a steak.

Irish Stew

½ cup water

¾ cup lamb, cut into 2-inch cubes

½ cup potato, sliced

½ cup carrots, sliced

¾ cup onions, sliced

½ cup green beans, chopped

1 clove garlic, minced

1 bay leaf (small)

¾ cup celery, sliced

¼ teaspoon dried rosemary

½ teaspoon dried mint

¼ teaspoon dried marjoram

2 tablespoons arrowroot

½ cup water

Carbohydrates	Grams
lamb	0.0
potato	12.8
carrots	7.0
onions	10.0
green beans	4.0
garlic	0.9
celery	4.0
arrowroot	14.0
Total	52.7
per serving	26.3

Bring water to a boil over medium heat. Add lamb, vegetables, and herbs, lower heat, and cook until meat is tender. Mix arrowroot with water and add to broth. Turn heat back up to medium. Move vegetables to sides of pan and stir arrowroot into broth. Continue to stir until sauce is thickened. Turn off heat and stir vegetables gently into sauce. Remove bay leaf. Serves 2.

Lamb Kabobs

Marinade:

1 tablespoon lemon juice

2 tablespoons olive oil

1 teaspoon dried or 1 tablespoon fresh rosemary or mint, crushed

1 clove garlic, crushed

Kabobs:

¾ cup onions, cut into quarters

¾ cup lamb, cut into 1-inch squares

½ cup green pepper, cut into 1-inch squares

¾ cup cherry tomatoes

½ cup zucchini, cut into 1-inch pieces

½ cup rice, cooked

¼ cup parsley, scissor-snipped

Carbohydrates	Grams
lemon juice	1.2
olive oil	0.0
herbs	0.8
garlic	0.9
onions	12.0
lamb	0.0
green pepper	1.9
tomato	7.5
zucchini	2.8
rice	19.1
parsley	1.4
Total	47.6
per serving	23.8

Marinate lamb squares for at least 3 hours in a glass or stainless steel dish in refrigerator, turning several times. Pour ¼ cup boiling water over onions to soften, if desired. Cut onion quarters in half again. Thread meat alternately with the vegetables onto skewers. Baste meat and vegetables with marinade. Broil for a short time so that meat remains rare and vegetables crunchy. In small saucepan, warm remainder of marinade. (It contains nutritious juices from the lamb.) Spoon rice onto two plates and pour marinade over rice, topping with sprinkling of parsley. Place kabobs on bed of rice. Serves 2.

NOTE: Cubes of fish, beef, or chicken liver may also be used. If chicken is used, be sure to cut it into thin strips and cook it until done.

Lamb Sausage

¼ teaspoon oregano or other herbs to taste

Carbohydrates	Grams
.........................negligible	

¼ teaspoon sage

¼ teaspoon thyme

1 clove garlic, pressed

2 tablespoons water

1 pound ground lamb or beef

Mix the spices into 2 tablespoons water. Knead this mixture into the ground meat and shape into patties. Broil or panfry patties to taste. Freeze any unused portions immediately.

Beef-Rutabaga Stew

¾ cup beef, cubed

½ cup water or broth

½ cup rutabaga, cut in half and thinly sliced

½ cup green beans or celery, sliced

½ cup onions, chopped

1½ cups cabbage, shredded

3 tablespoons parsley, snipped (optional)

½ teaspoon dried or 1 tablespoon fresh basil leaves

½ cup cooked rice (optional)

Salt or kelp as desired

Carbohydrates	Grams
beef	0.0
rutabaga	7.7
green beans	4.0
onions	7.0
cabbage	9.0
parsley	1.0
herbs	0.5
rice	19.1
Total	48.3
per serving	24.1

Put beef, water or broth, rutabaga, green beans, onions, and cabbage in pot. Cover with lid and bring just barely to a boil over medium heat. Reduce heat and simmer for 12 to 15 minutes, or until tender and crunchy. Turn off heat and stir in rice, herbs, and seasoning. Cover pot and allow stew to sit a few minutes. Serves 2.

Variation: Substitute any beans or other grain for rice, and experiment with all kinds of vegetables.

Chili Con Carne

1 or 2 cloves garlic, minced

¾ cup onions, chopped

¼ cup broth from beans or leftovers

1 cup beef, cut into cubes

1 cup cooked kidney beans

1 cup bell pepper, chopped

1 cup celery, including tops and outer stalks, chopped

2 tablespoons tomato paste (optional)

2 to 4 teaspoons chili powder

2 teaspoons cumin (optional)

1 teaspoon dried oregano (optional)

1½ cups tomatoes, chopped

2 tablespoons olive oil

Carbohydrates	Grams
garlic	1.8
onions	12.0
beef	0.0
beans	42.0
bell pepper	3.8
celery	5.0
tomato paste	6.0
herbs	4.5
tomatoes	15.0
olive oil	0.0
4 servings	90.1
per serving	22.5

Cook garlic and onions in broth over low heat until onions begin to soften. Add beef cubes and cook briefly. Add kidney beans, bell peppers, celery, and more liquid if desired. Cook until beef is tender. Stir in tomato paste, spices, and tomatoes and let warm. Stir in olive oil and let sit a few moments to blend flavors. Serves 3 or 4.

Variation: Sauté onions and garlic in 2 tablespoons butter and omit olive oil.

For a Balanced Meal: Serve with romaine lettuce salad and French dressing. Freeze any leftover chili for another time.

Tostadas

2 corn tortillas

1 cup lettuce, shredded, or alfalfa sprouts

¾ cup beef, cut into ½- or ¾-inch cubes and sautéed lightly

¾ cup tomato, chopped

¼ cup green onion, chopped

¼ cup cilantro leaves (optional)

½ cup cucumber, peeled and sliced

½ cup carrots, cut into strips

Carbohydrates	Grams
tortillas	27.0
lettuce	1.4
beef	0.0
tomato	7.5
green onion	2.0
cilantro	0.5
cucumbers	1.0
carrots	5.5
Total	45.7
per serving	22.8

Moisten tortillas in a little water, and warm in toaster oven. (Or you can warm tortillas with a little butter in a skillet over low heat.) Lay one tortilla on each plate. Spread lettuce over tortillas. Spoon beef, tomatoes, green onions, and cilantro over lettuce. Serve with cucumber slices and carrot strips. Serves 2.

Variation: You may add avocado slices or hot chili peppers to the tostada.

NOTE: *Candida* patients should limit themselves to one tortilla at a meal.

Kidney Stew

2 tablespoons butter

¼ teaspoon rosemary

¼ teaspoon marjoram

4 to 5 lamb kidneys,
thinly sliced

½ green pepper, sliced

½ onion, sliced

2 stalks celery, sliced

Extra broth, if necessary

1 tablespoon arrowroot to each
1½ cups broth

Carbohydrates	Grams
butter	2
herbs+kidneys	negligible
green pepper	2.0
onion	3.0
celery	4.0
arrowroot	7.0
Total	16.2
per serving	8.1

Melt butter and add rosemary and marjoram. Add kidneys, green pepper, onion, and celery. Stir-fry until warmed through (3 to 4 minutes). Add extra broth, if necessary. Mix arrowroot with a little water and add to broth. Continue stirring until clear. Season with herbed salt and serve. Serves 2.

Cooked Tongue

1 large calf or beef tongue, or
1 to 2 small lamb tongues per
person

Water to cover

8 peppercorns

2 medium onions, halved

4 carrots

Several celery tops

4 new potatoes or Jerusalem
artichokes

Carbohydrates	Grams
tongue	0.0
onions	12.0
carrots	30.0
celery	2.0
potatoes	45.0
Total	89.0
per serving	22.2

Place tongue in a Dutch oven. Add water and peppercorns to pot
and bring to a simmer (when the lid dances). Turn heat as low as
possible. Cook at low heat approximately 2 hours for beef
tongue, under 2 hours for lamb. Add all vegetables for the last
half hour of cooking, taking care not to overcook. Save the broth,
which is rich in minerals. Serves 4 or more, depending on the
size of the tongue.

SEAFOOD

The classical Chinese philosopher Lao-tzu said, "Ruling a large kingdom is like cooking a small fish." Both should be gently handled and their treatment never overdone!

Seafood is high in trace minerals and is an excellent source of protein. Fish from deep ocean waters are most desirable, as they are freer from pollutants than freshwater fish or scavengers. When shopping for fish, seek a local fish market. Fresh fish should have little or no odor and a bright sheen. The flesh should be firm, the eyes bulging. Fish on the bone retains more of its natural juices than when filleted. Culinary artist James Beard recommends cooking fish with its head and tail intact and claims it is more flavorful this way.[21]

Fresh fish is highly perishable. It must be used at once or frozen promptly. In freezing, place fish in a plastic bag and squeeze out as much air as possible to prevent dryness. Fish can be stored in the freezer of a refrigerator for only a week or two because such freezers are not sufficiently cold to prevent enzymatic changes that make nutritional value and flavor decline. If you have a deep freezer, remember that oily fish (such as salmon) do not store as long as other fish.

When thawing fish, allow about 8 hours per pound in the lower compartment of your refrigerator. A slow-thawing process will retain more of the natural juices. Pieces of frozen fish, which cook quickly, can be added to soups and stews.

Fish requires briefer cooking time than meats. The connective tissues of fish are delicate and break down quickly when heated. Because there is very little fat, heat penetrates more rapidly. Seasonings other than salt should be added at the beginning of the cooking process. A court bouillon (fish broth) can be prepared by lightly poaching a portion of fish seasoned with salt and other seasonings and then freezing the broth for later use.

Broiling is most appropriate for fish steaks or fillets (1 inch or more), approximately 5 minutes per side. Thinner pieces or fillets can be braised or poached in water or court bouillon. Poaching is most successful if the fish is placed over water on a flat steamer rack or wrapped in cheesecloth. This prevents the fish from flaking when removed from the broth.

To check for doneness, cut into the fish. No translucent flesh should be seen. Check about a minute before you think the fish will be done. If you wait until the fish falls apart at the touch of a fork, it will be overdone. If you are using a meat thermometer, the internal temperature should be 140° to 145°F.

Fish is often served with a sauce containing olive oil or avocado. Make your own tartar sauce or mayonnaise, or prepare a cooked sauce with sautéed herbed onions and garlic in butter.

Make a colorful fish entrée by shredding vegetables (carrots, onions, celery, and zucchini) into a Pyrex baking dish that has been lightly coated with olive oil. Place fish portions on top of this bed of vegetables, lightly brush the fish with herbed butter, and bake at 325°F until done.

Basic Poached Fish

This method of cooking fish is suggested for *Candida* patients. The fish is cooked at a low temperature, which yields a small quantity of delicious concentrated broth. If you do not use a vapor seal lid, increase the water in the recipe.

1 or 2 red snappers, whitefish, or bass fillets

Pinch thyme

2 tablespoons water or court bouillon

Lemon wedges

Carbohydrates	Grams
....................negligible	

Rinse fillets, pat dry, and season with thyme. Heat water over medium heat until water begins to bubble. Reduce heat and place fish in pot with water or court bouillon. Cover and simmer for 4 minutes, then turn fish and simmer 3 to 4 minutes on other side or until almost done. (Fish will continue to cook after being removed from the heat.) Serve with lemon wedges. Serves 2.

Variations: Complete fish with one of the following sauces:
- Curry Sauce (page 161)
- Tartar Sauce (page 174)
- Salsa de la Cocina (page 173)
- Quick Onion Sauce (page 172)

Easy Herbed Fish

This is a good way to prepare fish when you don't make a sauce.

1 tablespoon butter

½ teaspoon dried marjoram

½ pound fish (sole, cod, etc.)

Carbohydrates	Grams
butter	0.1
herb	0.5
fish	0.0
per serving	0.6

Melt butter over low heat. Stir in marjoram. Rinse fish and pat dry with paper towel. Coat both sides of fish with herbed butter and lay in pan. Simmer, covered, about 4 minutes for ⅜-inch-thick fish. Turn and simmer about 3 minutes. Check for doneness. Serves 1.

Fish in Butter-Ginger Sauce

⅔ cup Butter-Ginger Sauce
(see page 159)

⅔ pound fish (sole, cod, etc.)

Carbohydrates	Grams
sauce per serving	.........8.6
fish	.....................negligible

Prepare Butter-Ginger Sauce in saucepan over low heat so as to prevent butter from browning. Rinse fish and drain on paper towel. Lay fish over sauce. Cover pot and simmer a few minutes. Turn fish and cover with sauce. Simmer until almost done. (See instructions on checking for doneness, page 108.) Serves 2.

Sea Bass

2 sea bass steaks

Coconut butter

2 large or 4 small cloves garlic

1 lemon

Parsley, scissor-snipped

Carbohydrates	Grams
sea bass	0.0
coconut butter	0.0
garlic	1.5
lemon juice	1.5
parsley	0.5
Total	3.5

Sauté sea bass steaks in coconut butter with several slices (1 large or 2 small cloves) of garlic per steak. Add juice of lemon while cooking. When fish flakes easily with a fork, it is ready to serve with scissor-snipped parsley and a large green salad. Don't forget to check your Rainbow vegetable chart to add the variety of vegetables to your salad.

Brazilian Fish Bake

⅓ cup broth or water

2 tablespoons olive oil

½ potato, thinly sliced

½ carrot, thinly sliced

½ onion, thinly sliced

2 celery ribs, thinly sliced

¼ cup red bell pepper (about half a pepper), thinly sliced

2 fish fillets

Carbohydrates	Grams
broth or water	negligible
olive oil	0
potato	16
carrot	4
onion	5
celery	4
red bell pepper	1
fish fillets	0
Total	32

Pour broth or water with olive oil into bottom of casserole. Add vegetables. Arrange your fish fillets on top of the vegetables with a light coating of olive oil. Cover casserole and bake about 40 minutes at 350°F. You may substitute zucchini or chayote squash, leeks, tomatoes, and so forth, as long as you have each vegetable category in your combination.

Fish Cacciatore

¾ cup Cacciatore Sauce
(see page 160)

⅔ pound fish (sole, cod, etc.)

Carbohydrates	Grams
sauce per serving	........15.6
fish	...............negligible

Prepare sauce in saucepan. Rinse fish and pat dry with paper towel. Lay fish over sauce and cover pot. Simmer 3 to 4 minutes. Turn fish, cover with sauce, and simmer until just done. Serves 2.

Fish Chowder

3 to 4 tablespoons butter

½ cup leek or onion, minced

1 clove garlic, minced

½ cup carrots, thinly sliced

½ cup celery, thinly sliced

½ cup red potato, thinly sliced

2 cups broth (any kind you have on hand)

¼ cup parsley, chopped

½ bay leaf

1 whole clove

A few celery tops, chopped

¾ cup white fish (sole, bass, etc.) cut into cubes

⅛ teaspoon kelp

⅛ teaspoon Celtic sea salt (optional)

2 tablespoons parsley or chives, scissor-snipped

Carbohydrates	Grams
butter	0.4
onion	7.0
garlic	0.5
carrots	5.5
celery	2.3
potato	12.5
parsley, fish	1.2
Total	27.4
per serving	13.7

Melt butter over low heat and add minced leek or onion, garlic, carrots, celery, potato, and broth. Cover and simmer until vegetables are partially tenderized, about 5 minutes. Add parsley, bay leaf, clove, celery tops, and fish. Simmer 3 minutes more. Add kelp and salt. Remove bay leaf. Serve with snipped parsley or chives. Serves 2.

Italian Fish Stew (For Two)

Choose fish with a firm texture. Frozen fish with less attractive appearance than fresh fish may be used. Or you may use scraps, such as the meat from the jaws of the fish.

2 tablespoons butter

1 clove garlic, minced

½ cup onion, chopped

½ green pepper, chopped

1 cup celery, chopped

½ cup water or broth

¾ cup raw fish, cut into chunks

¾ cup very ripe tomato

½ cup parsley, coarsely chopped

¼ cup celery leaves, chopped

¼ teaspoon dried oregano

¼ teaspoon dried basil

¼ teaspoon dried thyme

Juice of 1 lemon or lime (optional)

Carbohydrates	Grams
butter	0.2
garlic	0.9
onion	7.5
green pepper	1.9
celery	6.3
fish	0.0
tomato	7.5
parsley	2.6
herbs	1.0
lemon juice	3.6
Total	31.5
per serving	15.8

Melt butter over low heat. Add garlic and onions and continue to cook over low heat, stirring occasionally, until softened. Stir in green pepper, celery, and broth. Continue to cook for 2 minutes. Add fish chunks and cook another few minutes, until fish is almost done. Add tomato, greens, and herbs and cook another 2 minutes. Fish should be cooked through but the vegetables should be still crisp and colorful. Remove from heat, cover, and let sit 3 to 5 minutes. Add lemon or lime juice and serve with yeast-free rye crackers. Serves 2 generously.

Variations: Stir in precooked beans or rice. Add ½ cup diced potatoes with onion and cook until soft. If potatoes are added, omit beans and rice.

Mock Tuna-Stuffed Tomato

This makes an attractive platter for a warm summer day luncheon.

Carbohydrates	Grams
fish	0.0
celery	5.7
parsley	3.7
onion	3.0
mayonnaise	0.5
tomatoes	14.0
Total	26.9
per serving	13.4

¾ cup fish, steamed and cooled

¾ cup celery, finely chopped

¾ cup parsley, minced

6 tablespoons green onion, minced

3 or 4 tablespoons Homemade Mayonnaise (see page 155)

½ teaspoon dried or 1 tablespoon fresh tarragon, snipped

2 tomatoes, cut into wedges

½ teaspoon dried or 1 tablespoon fresh dill weed, scissor-snipped

---

Flake fish and mix with chopped vegetables, mayonnaise, and tarragon. Arrange tomato wedges in a wheel on two plates. Spoon fish mixture over tomatoes. Garnish with fresh dill weed or lettuce. Serves 2.

Variations: Add carrot strips.

Stir cold cooked rice into the fish mixture or serve the salad with yeast-free rye crackers.

VEGETABLES

When purchasing vegetables, seek out the freshest possible, locally organically grown on good soil. Learn when produce is delivered to your market and plan your shopping accordingly. Select vegetables free of gene-altered and irradiated sources. Remember to always choose five vegetables to go with your complete protein and, if desired, your legume or grain. You need to choose a vegetable from each of these five categories:

1. A root vegetable (e.g., carrots, turnips, beets, etc.)
2. A yellow or white vegetable (e.g., cauliflower, cucumber, avocado, yellow squashes, etc.)
3. A green stalky veggie (e.g., asparagus, broccoli, celery, etc.)
4. A red, orange, or purple vegetable (e.g., pumpkin, sweet potato, purple cabbage, tomatoes, red peppers, etc.)
5. A green leafy vegetable (e.g., cabbage, lettuce, chard, greens-beet-turnip-mustard, kale, parsley, cilantro, etc.)

This variety of colors and textures provides you with a broad spectrum of desirable minerals and other factors.

Give carrots, beets, and squash the "pinch test," and reject any with soggy areas. Bypass cauliflower or broccoli that has any discolored or moldy areas. Avoid any potatoes that are green or sprouting due to overexposure to heat or light.

Seasonal produce will have the best flavor and be less expensive. Some additive-free frozen vegetables can be stocked for "emergencies," but plan to shop frequently for the fresh varieties in order to obtain optimal levels of needed vitamins and minerals.

Mold accumulates rapidly on surfaces whether food is refrigerated or not refrigerated. Wash vegetables before you use them rather than before storing them. Then scrub them with a stiff brush.

In storing greens, retain as much moisture in them as possible by dampening and then storing them leafy side down in plastic bags tied with a twister. Allow some air to remain inside of the bag before closing it to prevent the greens from becoming soggy.

Cut the leaves and stems from carrots and beets. This will prevent moisture and nutrients from being drawn out. Store the greens in separate bags. Store celery with a plastic bag protecting its green leaves. Zucchini and eggplant store best when left unwrapped in the refrigerator crisper drawer. Cauliflower stores best in a perforated wrapper that is kept slightly loose. Store onions, potatoes, yams, and winter squash in a cool cupboard with plenty of air circulation.

Scrub vegetables with a stiff brush before preparing. Avoid soaking, which results in the loss of nutrients in the water that is discarded. Do not peel vegetables if the peel is edible. It contains nutrients and dietary fibers. Nearly all vegetables except leafy greens can be saved for another recipe merely by cutting off the exposed ends before using them on another occasion. Three choices for cleansing soaks for your foods include:

1. Grapefruit seed extract (GSE) soak/rinse for vegetables, eggs, and so forth. Place 20 to 30 drops of GSE into a 1-quart spray bottle and fill with pure water. Spray foodstuffs with this mixture; it also may be used to wipe your kitchen counters and cutting boards. You may add the 20 to 30 drops

of GSE to a dishpan or sinkful of pure water and soak your produce in this, then rinse and spin-dry before storing in your refrigerator.

2. Add ½ teaspoon of Clorox (no substitutes!) to each gallon of water. After soaking, rinse or soak another 10 minutes in pure water, then drain or spin dry. Use at once or store for a short term in your refrigerator.

3. Add ¼ cup of 3 percent hydrogen peroxide to a sinkful of cold water. Soak leafy vegetables (lettuces, other salad greens) for 15 minutes; chicken, steaks, chops, roasts, fish, and eggs for 20 minutes; root vegetables (carrots, beets, potatoes) and other thick-skinned or stalky vegetables (celery, asparagus, green beans) for 30 minutes.

Grate, mash, or puree at the very last minute in order to prevent nutrient losses. As you become more experienced with minimal cooking times and use of very little liquid for cooking, you will better appreciate the brilliant colors and savory flavors in vegetable dishes.

For quick meals, you might like to use a Salad Shooter as a fast way to reduce the size of pieces of root vegetables (carrots, beets, potatoes, sweet potatoes, rutabagas, etc.) for rapid cooking (5 minutes or less) in your vegetable steamer basket.

Do not precook vegetables for future use; instead, cut the dense varieties into small pieces to cook in the same amount of time as other ingredients. Save the cooking liquids and add them to recipes requiring liquids, preserving the water-soluble nutrients.

For a quick, easy reference, we've classified vegetables according to their carbohydrate percentages.

Carbohydrate Percentage	Vegetables
3 percent	Asparagus, broccoli, cabbage, cauliflower, celery, cucumber, mustard greens, beet greens, turnip greens, chard, kale, zucchini, romaine lettuce, other leaf lettuces, spinach, summer squashes, radishes
6 percent	Bok choy, green beans, chives, tomatoes, eggplant, okra, red and yellow bell peppers, yellow wax beans, parsley, pumpkin, winter squash, turnips, pimiento
9 percent	Artichokes, beets, brussels sprouts, leeks, onions, rutabagas, carrots
15 percent	Various beans, parsnips, peas
18 percent	Horseradish, potatoes, sweet potatoes
21 percent	Fresh lima beans, fresh corn

Globe Artichokes

If you've never eaten an artichoke before, try it—it's fun! Just pull an outside artichoke leaf, dip in the butter, and pull the "meat" off the leaf with your teeth. When you reach the center, carefully remove and discard the thistles with a spoon and eat the heart.

Globe artichokes

1 lemon slice

Softened or melted butter or
Homemade Mayonnaise
(see page 155)

Carbohydrates	Grams
1 artichoke	9.9
mayonnaise	1.2
Total	11.1

Select artichokes with tightly closed leaves. Cut off stems, rinse well. Cover and cook in water with a lemon slice over low heat 30 to 40 minutes, depending on size. Stand the artichokes upright on plate and serve with a small cup of softened or melted butter, or Homemade Mayonnaise.

NOTE: In cooking for one, you may prefer to cook half an artichoke at a time. Simply cut it downward in half with a sharp knife and cook as above. In preparing a Super Seven Meal, tear off a handful of leaves at a time and cook them with the other vegetables. When you have used up all the outer leaves, cook the heart, remove and discard the delicate inner leaves and thistles, and then either eat the heart as is or put it in a salad.

Variation: Add lemon juice to melted butter.

Cauliflower-Eggplant Curry

1 tablespoon butter

½ teaspoon curry powder

1½ cups small cauliflower florets

1 cup eggplant, chopped

½ cup fresh peas

½ cup tomato, chopped

2 teaspoons lemon juice

2 tablespoons water (or more if not using vapor seal lid)

Carbohydrates	Grams
butter	0.1
curry	0.5
cauliflower	9.0
eggplant	8.0
peas	9.5
tomato	7.0
lemon juice	0.4
Total	34.5
per serving	17.2
Variation:	
rice, ½ cup	18.0
per serving	9.0

Melt butter over low heat and stir in curry powder. Add cauliflower and stir to coat. Add eggplant and peas. Add water and cover pot. Cook over medium heat just long enough to bring to a boil. Reduce heat and simmer until tender, about 8 minutes. Remove from heat and stir in tomatoes and lemon juice. Serves 2.

Variation: Substitute zucchini for eggplant; substitute green beans, cut into ½-inch pieces, for peas. Before adding tomato, stir in ½ cup cooked brown rice.

Crowned Eggplant

1 eggplant, sliced

1 large onion, thinly sliced

2 large tomatoes, sliced

1 cup parsley, finely minced

2 to 3 tablespoons fresh basil, minced (optional)

2 tablespoons butter

Carbohydrates	Grams
eggplant	16.0
onion	10.9
tomatoes	18.0
parsley, basil	5.1
butter	0.2
Total	50.2
per serving	8.4

Butter a cookie sheet and arrange eggplant slices on it. Place an onion slice and a tomato slice on each piece of eggplant. Add ½ teaspoon butter or less to each stack of vegetables. Bake at 350°F for 15 minutes or until fork-tender and soft. Garnish with herbs. A medium eggplant usually gives 12 slices or 6 servings. Prepare only the number of stacks of vegetables needed for one meal.

Baked "French Fries"

A delicious substitute for french fried potatoes.

1 medium potato

½ tablespoon butter or oil

Carbohydrates	Grams
potato	21.0
butter	0.0
per serving	10.5

Preheat over to 450°F. Scrub potato,
cut into slices, and then into ½-inch sticks, with skins retained.
Arrange in one layer in baking pan. Brush with melted butter or
oil. Bake for 15 minutes or until potato sticks are puffed and
golden brown. Serves 2.

Ratatouille

2 cloves garlic, minced

1 cup onions, chopped

2 tablespoons water (or more if needed)

2 cups eggplant, peeled and chopped

2 cups zucchini, chopped

1 cup bell pepper, chopped

¼ cup green onions, chopped

2 cups tomatoes, chopped

1 cup parsley, chopped

1 cup celery leaves, chopped

2 tablespoons tomato paste (optional)

½ teaspoon dried or
1 tablespoon fresh basil

½ teaspoon dried or
1 tablespoon fresh oregano

½ teaspoon dried or
1 tablespoon fresh thyme

2 tablespoons olive oil

Salt and/or kelp (optional)

Carbohydrates	Grams
garlic	1.8
onions	15.0
eggplant	14.8
zucchini	11.0
bell pepper	3.8
green onions	2.0
tomatoes	20.0
parsley	5.1
celery	5.0
tomato paste	12.2
herbs	1.5
olive oil	0.0
Total	92.2
per serving	15.7

Soften garlic and onions in water over low heat. (Increase water if not using waterless cookware.) Add eggplant and cook until it begins to soften. Add zucchini and cook until soft. Add bell pepper, green onions, tomatoes, parsley, celery leaves, tomato paste, and herbs and allow to warm. Add olive oil and let sit a few minutes. (If you like it soupier, add a little water or broth.) Serves 6.

Mock Spaghetti

1⅓ cups Cacciatore Sauce (see page 160, double quantity)

1 small spaghetti squash

Carbohydrates	Grams
Cacciatore Sauce (without tomato paste) 27.2	
(with tomato paste) 33.3	
spaghetti squash ....not available	

Fill pan with 1½ inches water and bring to a boil over medium heat. Meanwhile, cut squash lengthwise, and scoop out seeds. Place squash in pan, cut side down. Cover pot and simmer for 20 to 30 minutes, or until you can puncture squash with a fork. Remove from heat and pull pulp away from shell. It will look like spaghetti strings. Spoon Cacciatore Sauce over squash. Serves 2 generously.

Spaghetti Squash with Pesto

1 well washed and dried bunch parsley, cilantro, or basil, or one handful if fresh

¼ cup melted butter or ½ cup olive oil

2 or 3 cloves garlic

Strings from 1 spaghetti squash, cooked

⅓ cup pine nuts or other nuts

Carbohydrates	Grams
parsley or other greens	..10
butter, oil	0.0
garlic clove	0.9
spaghetti squash	10
nuts	12 to 15
Total	32.5

Place parsley, cilantro, or basil in your blender with melted butter or olive oil and garlic (to taste). Blend or food process to a puree. Mix gently into your spaghetti squash strings and toss as you would a salad. Add pine or other nuts as topping or mix into your serving dish.

SALADS

Brussels Sprouts Salad

This is a good balance of tender cooked and crunchy raw vegetables.

¾ cup brussels sprouts, quartered

¾ cup green beans, cut into ½-inch pieces

1 cup celery, chopped

½ cup bell pepper, chopped

2 tablespoons green onions, chopped

5 tablespoons olive oil

3 tablespoons lemon juice

2 tablespoons fresh or 1½ teaspoons dried basil

¾ cup parsley, chopped

Carbohydrates	Grams
brussels sprouts	7.5
beans	6.0
celery	6.0
bell pepper	1.9
green onions	0.8
lemon	3.6
parsley	4.0
Total	29.8
per serving	14.9
½ cup chickpeas add	30
½ cup cooked rice add	10

Cook brussels sprouts and green beans until tender but crunchy. Drain and chill 1 hour. Chop remaining vegetables and combine them with the cooked vegetables. Mix together olive oil, lemon juice, and herbs. Shake well and pour over salad. Toss to coat vegetables and chill 1 to 2 hours. Serves 2 generously.

Variation: Add either ½ cup cooked chickpeas or ½ cup cooked rice.

Caesar Salad

1 clove garlic, bruised

3 cups romaine lettuce, washed, dried, and torn

Salt to taste

¼ teaspoon dry mustard, or to taste

4 anchovy fillets, minced (optional)

Juice of 2 lemons

¼ cup olive oil

1 egg, poached

Carbohydrates	Grams
garlic	0.9
lettuce	6.0
lemon	4.8
egg	0.5
Total	12.2
per serving	6.1
Variation:	
½ cup rice add	19.1

Mash garlic with garlic press or with the flat side of a knife to release oils into salad bowl. Fill salad bowl with lettuce. Sprinkle with salt, dry mustard, and anchovies. Add lemon juice and olive oil. Break poached egg over salad. Toss gently until well mixed. Serves 2.

NOTE: *Candida* patients should not add croutons from yeasted bread. Substitute ½ cup cooked rice or millet or crumbs from a yeast-free bread.

Carrot-Cabbage Salad

This is a colorful salad that your guests will enjoy.

Ginger Dressing (see page 153)

1½ cups red cabbage, grated

1 cup carrots, grated

½ cup red bell pepper, grated

2 tablespoons green onions, chopped

Carbohydrates	Grams
Ginger Dressing	3.8
red cabbage	7.2
carrots	11.0
bell pepper	1.9
green onions	1.5
Total	25.4
per serving	12.7

Pour Ginger Dressing over vegetables and toss well. Serves 2.

Variation: This salad is also good with Green Goddess Dressing (see page 154).

Cauliflower-Egg Salad

2 tablespoons water

1½ cups cauliflower, cut very small

3 to 4 hard-cooked eggs, chilled (see page 40)

½ cup celery, chopped

¼ cup bell pepper, finely chopped

2 tablespoons green onions, finely chopped

½ cup parsley, minced

1 tablespoon thick Homemade Mayonnaise (see page 155)

½ teaspoon dried or 1 sprig fresh tarragon leaves

½ teaspoon dried or 1 tablespoon fresh dill weed

1 teaspoon lemon juice

Carbohydrates	Grams
cauliflower	9.0
eggs	1.5
celery	2.5
bell pepper	0.9
green onions	1.5
parsley	2.4
mayonnaise	negligible
herbs	1.0
lemon	0.5
Total	19.3

Bring 2 tablespoons water to a boil over medium heat and add cauliflower. Reduce heat, cover, and simmer until tender, 8 to 10 minutes. Drain cauliflower and chill in covered dish. Peel cooked eggs, dice, and chill in covered dish for about 1 hour. Prepare remaining vegetables and combine with chilled ingredients. Add mayonnaise and seasonings and toss. Serves 2.

Ginger Chicken Salad

This recipe is unusual because of the contrast of the warm chicken with the cool salad vegetables.

¼ cup Ginger Dressing
(see page 153)

2 tablespoons sesame seeds
(optional)

2 tablespoons butter

1 clove garlic, minced

1-inch cube ginger, grated

3 half chicken breasts, deboned

2 tablespoons water

3 cups lettuce, torn

1 cup Chinese cabbage, slivered

1 cup parsley, chopped

1 cup celery, sliced

¼ cup green onions, sliced

½ cup red cabbage, slivered

Carbohydrates	Grams
Ginger Dressing	4.6
sesame seeds	3.0
butter	0.2
garlic	0.9
ginger	1.3
chicken	0.0
lettuce	6.0
Chinese cabbage	2.3
parsley	5.1
celery	5.0
green onions	2.0
red cabbage	2.5
Total	32.9
per serving	8.1

Prepare Ginger Dressing and let sit. Spread sesame seeds out on a pan and toast in a 250°F oven about 30 minutes. Melt butter over low heat and sauté garlic and ginger. Cut chicken into bite-size pieces and sauté in butter. Add water, cover pot, and cook chicken over low heat until done. Chop vegetables into salad bowl. Add hot chicken to salad. Pour Ginger Dressing over salad and toss. Sprinkle hot sesame seeds over salad and serve at once. Serves 4.

Variations: Cooked peas, avocado cubes, or 1 cup of cooked rice may be added.

Cooked turkey can be sautéed for a few minutes and substituted for chicken. Try fish for contrast.

Red onion rings can be substituted for red cabbage.

Coleslaw

1½ cups green cabbage, grated or shredded

½ cup green pepper, chopped

½ cup carrots, grated

¼ cup green onions, chopped

3 or 4 tablespoons Homemade Mayonnaise (see page 155)

Dash lemon juice

¼ teaspoon celery seed or caraway seed, ground

Carbohydrates	Grams
cabbage	9.0
green pepper	1.9
carrots	5.5
green onions	1.6
mayonnaise	0.7
lemon	0.5
celery seed	1.5
Total	20.7
per serving	10.3

Combine prepared vegetables. Mix mayonnaise, lemon juice, and seasoning and pour over vegetables. Toss. Serves 2.

Variation: Add anise root slivers and omit celery and caraway seed from dressing.

Fish Salad

2 cups salad greens (lettuce, watercress, etc.)

½ cup carrots, grated

¼ cup bell pepper, diced

½ cup celery, sliced

¼ cup radishes, chopped

½ cup fish, cooked and chilled

2 to 3 tablespoons Homemade Mayonnaise (see page 155)

½ cup rice, cooked and chilled

Juice of ½ lemon

Carbohydrates	Grams
lettuce	4.0
carrots	5.5
bell pepper	0.9
celery	2.5
radishes	1.5
fish	0.0
mayonnaise	0.3
rice	20.0
lemon	2.5
Total	37.2
per serving	18.6

Layer greens and vegetables onto two plates. Mix fish with mayonnaise and add rice. Spoon over vegetables and toss lightly. Squeeze lemon juice over each. Serves 2.

Variations:
- Mix fresh herbs or curry powder into mayonnaise.
- Substitute avocado dressing for mayonnaise.
- Substitute any raw vegetables on hand for those listed above.
- Lightly cooked peas are especially good in salads.
- Substitute millet for rice, or omit the grain altogether.

Garden Luncheon Platter

This makes an attractive platter for a hot summer day.

On each plate arrange:

Carbohydrates	Grams
watercress 0.1	
asparagus......................2.0	
tomato 3.5	
eggs..............................0.8	
mayonnaise 0.4	
cucumber 1.0	
carrot 4.0	
celery 2.0	
parsley 0.2	
Total.............................14.0	
Variation:	
fish, add......................10.0	
substitutes, approximately same	

Several sprigs watercress

3 or 4 asparagus spears, cooked and cooled

½ tomato, cut into wedges

2 hard-cooked eggs, sliced in half lengthwise

2 tablespoons Homemade Mayonnaise (see page 155)

Cucumber strips

Carrot strips

Small celery stalks from celery heart, with leaves

Fresh chives, parsley, dill, or other herbs, scissor-snipped

Arrange first four ingredients on one side of plate and drizzle mayonnaise over them. Arrange finger vegetables on other side of plate. Sprinkle snipped herbs over mayonnaise. The above amounts will serve 1 person.

Variations: Place ¼ cup cooked, cooled rice in center of plate. Or substitute cooked flaked fish mixed with mayonnaise; substitute green onions for hard-cooked eggs. Substitute lightly cooked broccoli, cauliflower, or green beans for asparagus; spinach leaves or alfalfa sprouts for watercress, etc.

Green Salad

A reminder of how lovely a simple green salad can be for entertaining on a hot day.

6 medium-sized romaine leaves, torn

½ cup watercress, torn

½ cup cilantro or parsley, torn

¾ cup Chinese cabbage, slivered

½ cup celery, sliced diagonally

2 or 3 red onion rings, thinly sliced

½ avocado, sliced lengthwise (optional)

Olive oil

Lemon juice

Carbohydrates	Grams
lettuce	1.0
watercress	1.1
parsley	2.4
cabbage	1.5
celery	2.3
onions	1.5
avocado	6.0
lemon	2.0
Total	17.8
per serving	8.9

Prepare greens in a salad bowl. Add celery and toss. Garnish with onion and avocado. Add olive oil and lemon juice or other favorite dressing. Serves 2.

Jane's Salad

This salad is attractive when placed on a bed of whole lettuce leaves, garnished with 2 or 3 tomato wedges on the side.

¾ cup cooked turkey, shredded or chopped

½ cup fresh peas, lightly cooked

½ cup celery, chopped

½ cup cauliflower, pulled apart or cut into small pieces

1 tablespoon red onion, chopped

¼ cup parsley, chopped

1 cup lettuce, chopped

Carbohydrates	Grams
turkey	0.0
peas	10.0
celery	2.5
cauliflower	3.0
onion	1.0
parsley	1.2
lettuce	2.0
Total	19.7
per serving	9.8

Toss with Homemade Mayonnaise (see page 155) or other dressing. Serves 2.

Variation: If red onion is unavailable, garnish with bits of red pepper or red cabbage.

Mexican Salad

¾ cup beef, broiled and cut into ½-inch squares

1½ cups lettuce, torn

¾ cup tomato, chopped

¾ cup celery, chopped

½ cup green onions, chopped

½ cup cucumber, peeled and chopped

¼ cup fresh cilantro

½ cup avocado, chopped

½ cup pinto beans, cooked and cooled

½ teaspoon chili powder, or to taste

1 tablespoon olive oil

Juice of ½ lemon or lime

Carbohydrates	Grams
beef	0.0
lettuce	3.0
tomato	7.5
celery	3.5
green onions	3.0
cucumber	2.0
cilantro	1.2
avocado	8.0
beans	30.0
olive oil	0.0
lemon	2.5
Total	60.7
per serving	30.3

Combine beef and chopped vegetables in an attractive serving dish. Sprinkle chili powder over salad. Pour oil and juice over salad. Toss well. Serves 2.

Variation: Add chili peppers if desired.

Mint-Pea Salad

¼ cup green onions, minced

½ cup peas, fresh or frozen

3 cups loosely packed lettuce, finely torn

1 cup celery, sliced

½ cup loosely packed fresh mint leaves, scissor-snipped

2 teaspoons olive oil

2 teaspoons lemon juice

Carbohydrates	Grams
green onions	2.0
peas	10.0
lettuce	6.0
celery	4.0
mint	1.0
olive oil	0.0
lemon	1.0
Total	24.0
per serving	12.0

Cook onions and fresh peas in a little water over low heat until they are soft. (If you use frozen peas, defrost and use as they are.) Remove onion and peas from cooking water and let cool. Make a bed of torn lettuce on each plate. Add sliced celery, peas, onions, and mint leaves. Spoon mixed oil and lemon juice over each plate. Serves 2.

Oriental Salad

¾ cup chicken, cooked, cooled, and cut into cubes

½ cup bell pepper, slivered

½ cup snow peas

½ cup celery, slivered

½ cup bean sprouts

1 cup watercress or parsley, chopped

½ cup jicama, cut into strips

Ginger Dressing (see page 153)

Carbohydrates	Grams
chicken	0.0
bell pepper	1.9
peas	10.0
celery	2.0
sprouts	2.5
watercress	5.0
jicama	12.8
Ginger Dressing	3.8
Total	38.0
per serving	19.0

Put chicken and vegetables in salad bowl. Pour Ginger Dressing over salad and toss. Serves 2.

Variation: Substitute Jerusalem artichokes or canned water chestnuts for jicama. Garnish with sesame seeds.

Armenian Salad

3 cucumbers

3 ribs of celery

12 radishes

¼ cup pine nuts

Cherry tomatoes

Parsley

2 tablespoons lemon juice

Olive oil

Celtic sea salt

Papaya pepper

Carbohydrates	Grams
cucumbers	7
celery	6
radishes	3
pine nuts	6
lemon juice	2
olive oil	0
Celtic sea salt and pepper	negligible
Total	24

Dice cucumbers, slice stalks of celery, and slice radishes; add pine nuts. Garnish with cherry tomatoes and parsley. Dress with lemon juice, olive oil, Celtic sea salt, and papaya pepper to taste.

Curried Rice Salad

½ cup cooked rice

½ cup cooked peas (or defrosted frozen peas)

1 cup celery, sliced

2 tablespoons green onion, chopped

½ cup bell pepper, chopped

½ cup carrots, sliced

¼ cup Homemade Mayonnaise (see page 155)

1 teaspoon curry powder, or to taste

Carbohydrates	Grams
rice	18.5
peas	10.0
celery	6.0
green onion	1.0
bell pepper	1.9
carrots	8.0
mayonnaise	0.6
curry powder	1.0
Total	47.0
per serving	23.5

Mix all ingredients well. Let sit a few minutes to blend the flavors. Serves 2.

Variation: Rice cooked in broth adds extra flavor to the salad. Use lightly cooked vegetables if desired. Add or substitute other vegetables, such as Jerusalem artichokes, water chestnuts, tomatoes, or zucchini.

Zucchini Salad

½ cup coconut cream

2 tablespoons lemon or lime juice

Few drops stevia

3 small young zucchinis (about 1 pound), shredded

3 scallions, finely minced, including roots and tops

2 tablespoons parsley, chopped

2 tablespoons red or yellow bell pepper, shredded

Carbohydrates	Grams
coconut cream	trace
lemon juice	2.0
stevia	0.0
zucchini	6.0
scallions	1.5
parsley	1.0
bell pepper	0.5
Total	12.0

Combine coconut cream, lemon or lime juice, and stevia, and mix with the vegetables. Refrigerate at least 30 minutes before serving to allow the flavors to blend. Serve with lettuce and avocado.

Steak Salad

½ cup broiled beef (rib steak, etc.), cut into cubes

2 cups lettuce (romaine, etc.), torn, or alfalfa sprouts

½ cup or less rice, cooked and cooled (optional)

½ cup raw carrot, grated

½ cup radishes, sliced

½ cup snow peas

½ cup cucumber, peeled and sliced

Basic French Dressing (see page 150)

¼ teaspoon dry mustard

Salt or kelp (optional)

Carbohydrates	Grams
beef	0.0
lettuce	4.0
rice	19.1
carrot	5.5
radishes	2.0
snow peas	4.0
cucumber	1.8
Basic French Dressing	2.6
Total	39.0
per serving	19.5

Chill meat 1 hour. Make a bed of torn lettuce on each plate. Sprinkle rice over lettuce, followed by grated carrot. Add radishes, snow peas, cucumber, and meat. Serve with Basic French Dressing with ¼ teaspoon of dry mustard added.

Variations: You can substitute any vegetables you like. Tomatoes, bell pepper, celery, onions, peas, and artichoke hearts would be excellent choices.

Tabouli

A grain salad from the Middle East.

½ cup boiling water

¼ cup bulgur wheat

½ cup green onions, chopped

1 cup parsley, chopped

½ cup bell pepper, chopped

1½ cups tomato, chopped

1½ cups celery, chopped

¼ cup fresh mint leaves, finely chopped

2 tablespoons olive oil

¼ cup lemon juice, or to taste

Salt (optional)

Kelp (optional)

Carbohydrates	Grams
bulgur	21.2
onions	7.5
parsley, mint, oil	5.0
bell pepper	1.9
tomato	15.2
celery	7.5
lemon juice	4.8
Total	63.1
per serving	15.7

Pour water over the bulgur and let stand for 2 hours until light and fluffy. Remove excess water by draining through a strainer or squeezing with your hands. Mix bulgur with chopped vegetables and mint. Add oil, lemon juice, salt, and kelp, and chill 1 hour. Serve with meat, fish, or eggs for a balanced meal. Serves 4.

NOTE: Bell pepper and celery are not customarily included in tabouli. If omitted, increase the quantity of other vegetables.

Rainbow Coleslaw

1 tablespoon Homemade
Mayonnaise (see page 155)

1 tablespoon coconut cream

1 scallion, well washed, roots
and leaves as well, minced

1½ cups green cabbage, shredded

1½ cups red cabbage, shredded

¼ cup red bell pepper, diced

¼ cup yellow bell pepper, diced

½ cup carrot, shredded

Carbohydrates	Grams
mayonnaise	trace
coconut cream	trace
scallion	0.5
red and green cabbage	15
red and yellow bell peppers	1.9
carrot	1.5
Total	19.0

Mix mayonnaise and coconut cream in serving bowl. Add
vegetables and toss to coat all of them with the dressing. Let chill
while covered for at least 20 minutes in the refrigerator to allow
flavors to blend. Serves 1.

DRESSINGS

Anchovy Dressing

1 can of anchovies in olive oil

1 cup olive oil

1 clove garlic, minced

¼ cup lemon juice

¼ cup cooked beets (optional)

Carbohydrates	Grams
anchovies	trace
olive oil	trace
garlic	0.9
lemon juice	4.8
beets	3.1
per 1½ cups	8.8
per ⅛ cup serving	0.7

Puree ingredients in blender. Makes
1½ cups. Use over salads.

Avocado Salad Dressing

1 ripe avocado

1 clove garlic, minced

1 tablespoon fresh lemon juice

Salt and/or kelp

Herbal seasoning

Carbohydrates	Grams
avocado	12.6
garlic	0.9
lemon juice	1.2
per ½ cup	14.7
per ⅛ cup	3.7

Blend all ingredients on low speed until
smooth and serve over salad. Makes about ½ cup.

Variation: Add Homemade Mayonnaise (see page 155) to taste for a creamy consistency and 1 or 2 teaspoons grated onions. Thin this dressing with 1 or 2 tablespoons of olive oil, if desired. Add chopped tomato.

Creamy Cucumber Dressing

¼ cup Homemade Mayonnaise (see page 155)

½ cup cucumber, peeled and cut into chunks

½ teaspoon dried or 1 tablespoon fresh tarragon leaves

½ teaspoon dried dill or 1 tablespoon fresh dill leaves

½ teaspoon dry mustard

1 teaspoon lemon juice

Carbohydrates	Grams
mayonnaise	0.6
cucumber	1.8
herbs	1.0
lemon juice	0.4
Total	3.8
per serving	1.9

Blend on low speed in blender. Let sit a few minutes. Pour over salad. Serves 2.

Basic French Dressing

3 tablespoons olive oil

1 tablespoon lemon juice

1 clove garlic, crushed

1 pinch dried tarragon or at least
1 teaspoon fresh tarragon leaves

1 pinch dried or 1 teaspoon
fresh thyme leaves

Pinch salt

Dash kelp

Carbohydrates	Grams
olive oil	0.0
lemon juice	1.2
garlic	0.9
herbs	0.5
per ¼ cup	2.6

Mix well and pour over salad. Makes ¼ cup.

Variations: French dressing is traditionally made with 3 parts oil
to 1 part vinegar. *Candida* patients need to substitute lemon
juice for vinegar. You can adjust the amount of lemon juice
according to your taste.

Substitute any herbs you prefer. Or use an herbed
seasoning salt to replace salt and herbs.

If you cannot tolerate citrus fruit such as lemon juice,
substitute a little powdered vitamin C dissolved in water.

Easiest-Ever French Dressing

If you've been pouring commercially prepared dressing over your salad, you may believe that making homemade French dressing is bothersome. If so, the following method will change your belief. After you've made it once or twice and learned to judge quantities, you'll discover that it's really easy, and there's no jar to wash.

Per Person:

    1 tablespoon olive oil

    1 teaspoon lemon juice

    Pinch each dried tarragon or other herbs, dried thyme, salt, and kelp

Carbohydrates	Grams
olive oil	0.0
lemon juice	0.4
herbs	0.5
Total	0.9

Measure oil and lemon juice and pour into bottom of salad bowl. Toss in herbs and seasonings. Blend with a fork. Add torn lettuce and other salad vegetables. When ready to serve, toss well.

NOTE: You can also pour the ingredients over the salad and toss. However, the above method allows the herbs to release their flavor into the dressing.

Garbanzo Dressing

Create a tasty dressing from beans, and use it in place of your bean or grain portion. Bean dressings are high in carbohydrates. Limit portions.

¼ cup garbanzo beans (chickpeas), cooked

¾ cup parsley, chopped

1 tablespoon green onion, chopped

2 tablespoons cooking water from garbanzo beans

2 tablespoons olive oil

1 teaspoon lemon juice

¼ teaspoon dried or 1 tablespoon fresh basil leaves

Carbohydrates	Grams
garbanzos	15.0
parsley	4.0
green onion	0.5
olive oil	0.0
lemon juice	1.2
herbs	0.3
Total	21.0
per serving	10.5

Puree at low speed in blender. Pour over salad. Serves 2.

Ginger Dressing

3 tablespoons olive oil

1 to 2 tablespoons lemon juice

1 teaspoon ginger, freshly grated

1 clove garlic, minced

Carbohydrates	Grams
olive oil	0.0
lemon juice	2.4
ginger	0.5
garlic	0.9
Total	3.8

Mix and let sit a few minutes. Pour over salad or cooked vegetables. Makes ¼ cup.

Green Goddess Dressing

¼ cup Homemade Mayonnaise (see page 155)

1 tablespoon each parsley, chives or green onion, fresh dill leaves (or ½ teaspoon dried dill weed), scissor-snipped

1 to 2 teaspoons lemon juice

1 to 2 teaspoons olive oil

Carbohydrates	Grams
mayonnaise	0.6
parsley	0.6
chives	0.6
lemon juice	0.8
olive oil	0.0
Total	2.6
per serving	1.3

Mix ingredients, using additional lemon juice and olive oil to thin dressing as desired. Let sit a few minutes. Pour over raw or cooked vegetables. Serves 2.

Variation: Add 1 or 2 chopped anchovy fillets.

Homemade Mayonnaise

Make your own mayonnaise and omit both vinegar and sugar. Basic mayonnaise can be used alone or herbs may be added to make all sorts of dressings for salads, vegetables, and fish.

Making mayonnaise is quite simple, although cookbooks caution about how it may curdle and offer remedies for rescuing it in such an event. As long as you drizzle the oil into the blender slowly while it whirs, you'll have no problem.

1 egg

2 tablespoons lemon juice

1 cup olive oil

1 teaspoon mustard (optional)

¼ teaspoon powdered kelp (optional)

¼ teaspoon salt (optional)

Carbohydrates	Grams
egg	0.5
lemon juice	2.4
oil	trace
seasoning	1.7
Total	4.6

Beat egg in blender on low speed. Then add lemon juice and seasoning if desired. Continue to blend and slowly drizzle in oil. Continue blending until smooth. Makes 1½ to 2 cups. Stores for 2 to 3 days in the refrigerator.

Creamy Tomato Dressing

2 tablespoons Homemade
Mayonnaise (see page 155)

⅓ cup tomato, chopped

2 teaspoons lemon juice

⅛ teaspoon dried or 1 teaspoon
fresh basil

Carbohydrates	Grams
mayonnaise	0.4
tomato	3.3
lemon juice...................	0.8
Total............................	4.5

Blend on low speed in blender. Makes about ⅓ cup.

Fresh Tomato Dressing

1 cup tomatoes, chopped

2 tablespoons lemon juice

½ teaspoon kelp

1 clove garlic, minced

1 tablespoon fresh basil,
oregano, or mint

⅛ teaspoon Celtic sea salt

½ teaspoon fresh horseradish,
grated

Carbohydrates	Grams
tomatoes	10.0
lemon...........................	2.2
kelp, herbs	0.0
garlic	0.9
horseradish...................	0.2
Total............................	13.3

Blend on low speed in blender. Pour over salad greens. Makes ½
cup.

Lemon/Oil Salad Dressing

1 large clove garlic, or
2 small cloves, crushed

¼ cup organic extra virgin olive
oil

1½ tablespoons lemon juice

½ teaspoon dry mustard, or
freshly ground mustard seed

Celtic sea salt to taste

Carbohydrates	Grams
garlic	0.9
olive oil	0
lemon juice	1.5
mustard	0
Celtic sea salt	0

Mix ingredients in a blender or use a whisk in a small bowl.

Sesame Seed Dressing

¼ cup raw mechanically hulled
sesame seeds

⅛ to ¼ cup organic extra virgin
olive oil

Juice of 1 lemon or lime

Pure water as needed

Carbohydrates	Grams
sesame seed	7
olive oil	0
lemon juice	3
pure water	0
Total	10

Place first three ingredients into blender and blend at slowest
speed. It will get thick immediately. Slowly add water until it has
a thin dressing consistency suitable for your use. Add garlic
and/or other fresh scissor-snipped herbs as desired.

Papaya Seed Dressing

2 tablespoons fresh or
1 tablespoon home-dried
papaya seeds

Several drops (2 to 7 or to taste)
stevia extract

½ medium onion (Maui onion if
you can find it)

½ teaspoon Celtic sea salt

½ teaspoon poupon mustard,
or more to taste

¼ cup freshly squeezed lemon
juice, or to taste

1⅓ cups organic extra virgin
olive oil

1 teaspoon freshly grated ginger
root (optional)

Carbohydrates	Grams
papaya seeds	..not available
stevia	0
onion	4
Celtic sea salt	0
mustard	0
lemon juice	4.4
ginger root	0.5
Total	10

Blend all ingredients until smooth. Keep refrigerated in small
4-ounce jars. It is delicious over fresh greens such as lettuce,
chicory, Belgian endive, New Zealand spinach, and sprouts.

SAUCES

Butter-Ginger Sauce

This sauce is especially good over fish, cooked carrots, and zucchini.

1 cup onions, chopped

1 clove garlic, minced

2 tablespoons butter

1 teaspoon ginger, freshly grated

2 teaspoons lemon juice
(optional)

Carbohydrates	Grams
onions	15.0
garlic	0.9
butter	0.1
ginger	1.3
lemon juice	0.6
Total	17.9
per ⅓ cup	8.9

Simmer onions and garlic in butter until soft. Stir in ginger and lemon juice. Makes ⅔ cup.

Cacciatore Sauce

This sauce is good for fish, chicken, eggs, and vegetables, especially zucchini and green beans.

1 tablespoon butter

½ cup onions, chopped

¼ cup green pepper, chopped

1½ cups tomato, chopped

½ cup parsley, chopped

1 tablespoon tomato paste (optional)

½ teaspoon dried basil or
1 tablespoon fresh basil leaves

½ teaspoon dried oregano or
1 tablespoon fresh oregano

Carbohydrates	Grams
butter	0.1
onions	7.5
green pepper	1.0
tomato	15.0
parsley	2.6
tomato paste	3.0
herbs	1.0
per ¾ cup	30.2

Melt butter over low heat. Add vegetables, tomato paste, and herbs, and simmer until sauce is reduced to ¾ cup.

Curry Sauce

2 tablespoons butter

¼ cup onions, chopped

1 clove garlic, minced

1 inch piece ginger root, grated

¼ cup celery, chopped

¼ cup bell pepper, chopped

2 rounded tablespoons arrowroot

3 cups broth, or soup stock seasoned to taste

1 tablespoon curry powder

Seasoning salt to taste

Carbohydrates	Grams
butter	0.2
onions	3.7
garlic	0.9
ginger	1.3
celery	1.1
bell pepper	0.9
arrowroot	14.0
curry	3.0
Total	25.1
per ½ cup	4.1

Melt butter over low heat. Add onions, garlic, and ginger, and cook until softened. Add celery and bell pepper, cover, and simmer for a few minutes. Mix arrowroot in ½ cup broth and stir into vegetables. Add remaining broth and heat, stirring over medium heat, until the mixture begins to boil. Reduce heat and simmer, stirring constantly, until sauce is clear and thick. Add curry powder and seasoning salt. Serve over rice, diced meats, vegetables, etc. Makes 3 cups.

Basic Pesto

3 cloves garlic, or to taste

2 cups fresh basil leaves

¼ cup pine nuts or walnuts

Scant teaspoon Celtic sea salt

¼ teaspoon papaya pepper

¾ cup organic extra virgin olive oil (divided use)

Carbohydrates	Grams
garlic	2.7
basil	not available
nuts	6
Celtic sea salt	0
papaya pepper	trace
olive oil	0
Total	8.7

Puree garlic, basil, nuts, and seasonings in blender with half the amount of olive oil, slowly adding the remaining half of olive oil. Place in lidded jar to protect from air, which will turn the pesto brown if it is not protected.

Cilantro Pesto

2 large handfuls cilantro (about 2 cups)

¾ cup organic extra virgin olive oil

⅓ cup pine nuts, walnuts, or almonds

4 to 6 cloves garlic, or
1 clove elephant garlic, peeled

¼ teaspoon Celtic sea salt

Carbohydrates	Grams
cilantro	10
olive oil	0.0
nuts	12 to 15
garlic (per clove)	0.9
Total	32.5

Place cilantro in a blender or food processor with part of the oil, blend to chop, add nuts and remaining oil while slowly blending. This may be made using just the cilantro, olive oil, and a little Celtic sea salt for a simpler pesto. This can be enjoyed with steamed spaghetti squash and a few additional pine nuts, or with any lightly steamed vegetable. Serve with a large mixed raw vegetable salad, as well as a protein source.

Garlic Spread

¼ pound butter, softened at
room temperature

¼ cup olive oil

4 garlic cloves, peeled (vary
amount according to your taste
preference)

Carbohydrates	Grams
butter	0.8
olive oil	0.0
garlic	3.6
Total	4.4

Blend in 8-ounce canning jar with Osterizer cutting base in
place. Store in refrigerator. Enjoy on steamed vegetables, or use
to gently sauté meats, fish, or vegetables.

Mint Sauce

3 tablespoons finely cut fresh
mint leaves

½ teaspoon Celtic sea salt

1 tablespoon fresh lemon or lime
juice

2 or more drops stevia liquid
extract

Carbohydrates	Grams
mint ....negligible
Celtic sea salt 0
lemon juice 1
stevia 0
Total 1

Blend all ingredients in mini 4-ounce jar. Serve with lamb.

Fresh Horseradish

1 piece horseradish root

1 tablespoon lemon juice

1 tablespoon coconut cream
(optional)

Carbohydrates	Grams
horseradish	3
lemon juice	1
coconut cream..................	1
Total	5

Scrub horseradish root well with a brush, and use one of the
vegetable soaks (see pages 119–120) for the root, which should
be thinly sliced into a 4-ounce jar for your blender. Add lemon
juice and, if you like, 1 tablespoon of coconut cream. Blend.
Enjoy carefully, as it is *hot!* Delicious with lamb!

Mustard

3 tablespoons mustard seeds
(available from your local health
food store)

2 tablespoons lemon juice
(optional)

⅛ teaspoon ascorbic acid powder

Carbohydrates	Grams
mustard seed	unknown
lemon juice	2
ascorbic acid powder	unknown
Total	2+

Soak mustard seeds overnight in pure water and drain. Rinse
and drain several times throughout the day. Grind the soaked,
semi-sprouted seeds in a 4-ounce blender jar with lemon juice
(or 2 tablespoons pure water) and ascorbic acid powder. Again,
this is hot! Taste judiciously!

Mock Hollandaise Sauce

1 egg

¼ teaspoon seasoning salt

¼ teaspoon dulse or kelp

1 tablespoon lemon juice

½ stick butter (¼ cup)

¼ cup hot water

Carbohydrates	Grams
egg	0.5
lemon juice	1.2
butter	0.4
1 cup	2.1
¼ cup serving	0.5

Blend the first five ingredients until smooth. While blending on low speed, carefully add hot water. Stir over boiling water until thick. Makes about 1 cup.

Italian Marinade

3 tablespoons olive oil

3 tablespoons lemon juice

¼ tablespoon dried or
1 tablespoon fresh oregano

¼ teaspoon dried or 1 tablespoon
fresh thyme

1 slice onion (optional)

1 clove garlic (optional)

Carbohydrates	Grams
olive oil	0.0
lemon juice	3.6
herbs	0.0
onion	0.6
garlic	0.9
Total	5.1

Blend olive oil, lemon juice, and herbs with a fork. Add onion and garlic. Makes about ⅓ cup.

Lemon Marinade

6 tablespoons olive oil

3 tablespoons freshly squeezed lemon juice

3 tablespoons fresh parsley, chopped

1 tablespoon fresh chives, chopped

1 teaspoon onion, grated

1 clove garlic, minced

¼ teaspoon cumin seed, crushed

¼ teaspoon salt or kelp

⅛ teaspoon dry mustard

Carbohydrates	Grams
olive oil	0.0
lemon juice	3.6
parsley	1.0
chives	0.5
onion	1.0
garlic	0.9
herbs	0.7
Total	7.7

Place all ingredients in small bowl or jar and stir or shake to mix well. Makes about ⅔ cup.

Lemon Sauce

This delicate sauce can be made from your vegetable steaming water. (Avoid using steaming water with strongly flavored vegetables such as cabbage.)

1 tablespoon arrowroot

2 tablespoons cool water

1 teaspoon lemon rind, grated

1 egg yolk

2 tablespoons lemon juice

⅔ cup vegetable broth

Carbohydrates	Grams
arrowroot	.....................7.0
lemon rind	..................0.3
lemon juice	..................2.4
egg yolk	........................0.1
Total	............................9.8
per serving	.................4.9

Dissolve arrowroot and water in a small cup. Grate lemon rind and set aside. In a small bowl, beat egg yolk and lemon juice with fork. Add arrowroot mixture to vegetable broth and cook over medium heat until clear. Beat 3 tablespoons of this mixture, one after another, into lemon-yolk mixture and then combine with the rest of the vegetable broth. Add lemon rind. Simmer and stir constantly for 4 to 5 minutes. Makes about 1 cup.

Variations: Pour sauce over cauliflower, fish, or chicken for a deliciously flavored dish.

Quick Onion Sauce

Onions can be used in a sauce to replace white or root vegetables in the Rainbow Meal Plan.

Carbohydrates	Grams
butter	0.2
onions	7.5
Total	7.7
per serving	3.9

2 tablespoons butter

½ cup onions, chopped

Melt butter over low heat. Simmer onions in butter until soft. Spoon over cooked vegetables, fish, or brown rice. Serves 2.

Variations:
- Add ½ cup finely minced parsley.
- Add ½ teaspoon dried thyme or other favorite herbs, as desired.

Salsa de la Cocina

This is a good sauce to have available for fish or scrambled eggs. You can prepare it ahead and freeze it in small packages.

2 cups tomatoes or tomatillos, cut into pieces

1 small chili (½ if very hot) (optional)

1 cup cilantro (optional)

½ cup onions, chopped

½ cup bell pepper, chopped

½ teaspoon kelp

Celtic sea salt (to taste)

Carbohydrates	Grams
tomatoes	20.0
chili	0.5
cilantro	3.0
onions	7.5
bell pepper	1.9
kelp	0.9
Total	33.8
per ¼ cup serving	2.8

Combine ingredients and serve, or chill if desired. Makes 3 cups, twelve ¼-cup servings.

Variations:
- Add ½ cup chopped parsley.
- If cilantro is unavailable, add ½ teaspoon ground coriander seed.
- For a different texture, you can puree ingredients at low speed in a blender briefly.

Tartar Sauce

½ cup Homemade Mayonnaise (see page 155)

1 to 2 tablespoons green onions or fresh chives, scissor-snipped

1 teaspoon lemon juice

1 teaspoon dried tarragon or 1 tablespoon fresh tarragon, scissor-snipped

1 teaspoon dried dill weed or 1 tablespoon fresh dill weed, scissor-snipped

Carbohydrates	Grams
mayonnaise	1.2
green onions	1.0
lemon juice	0.3
herbs	0.6
Total	3.1
per serving	1.5

Mix with a fork and let sit while you prepare fish. Serves 2.

Variation: Add 2 tablespoons finely chopped canned olives. Be sure to use a brand that has no additives.

CHEATS AND TREATS

We all cheat on occasion, but should not indulge too often. We should try to have rare splurges in the least harmful way possible. Some of the following suggestions stretch the health rules a little but will offer something different for the occasional infraction of your diet.

Try a small handful of raw almonds or sunflower seeds. Soak them overnight to soften them. A combination of sunflower, pumpkin seeds, and almonds is more textured and nutritious than the nuts or seeds by themselves.

Experiment with 1-inch squares or thin slices of Essene Bread[22] (made from sprouted grain without yeast) toasted with butter. Limit your consumption of these goodies.

Make a batch of Millet Muffins (see page 84). Indulge in one, and freeze the rest. Try the Oat Bran-Sweet Potato Muffins (see page 86).

Check the carbohydrate charts and choose the *least* harmful indulgences. If you crave fresh fruits, choose those with the lowest amounts of carbohydrates—for example, strawberries rather than bananas; or fresh or frozen strawberries with whipping cream rather than strawberry ice cream. (See Carbohydrate Chart, pages 204–211.)

Above all, remember that your goal is renewed health. It is just not worthwhile to dig into the "sugar barrel." Keep patting yourself on the back mentally and encourage yourself by remembering how well you are doing. If you cheat, however, do not feel guilty. Forgive yourself, and continue with even greater resolve to adhere to the diet.

A good low-heat dehydrator (one that can operate at temperatures of 98° to 99°F) can be a great help in preparing snacks for the Rainbow Meal Plan. Try to have whatever you choose to dehydrate sliced as thinly as possible to facilitate the removal of the moisture. I find that almost everything I dehydrate is dry and crisp enough in just under twenty-four hours of drying time.

When eating dehydrated foods or taking powdered food supplements, one should drink extra water. The amount of extra water should be equivalent to what was removed by the dehydrating process, to facilitate the food's rehydration and digestion, as well as its absorption into our bodies.

Baked Beets

This is an unusual dessert, and delicious.

1 medium or ½ large beet per person

Whipped cream

Carbohydrates	Grams
⅓ cup beets	4.1
cream	0.8
per serving	4.9

Scrub the beets. Preheat oven to 375°F. Leave skins on. Bake in Pyrex baking dish for 45 minutes. Remove and allow the beets to cool just enough to handle with some old pot holder that is ready to be discarded. Grate the beets, using the large holes on the grater. (The skin will not go through the holes.) Place about ⅛ of grated beet in each sherbet glass, and top with ⅛ cup of whipped cream per serving.

Variation: Serve the cream unwhipped over the grated beets.

Carrot Puff

It's pleasant to have a treat now and then! This is a good dessert dish for occasional use. The carrots are cooked a long time.

2 cups carrots, finely diced

2 tablespoons butter

1 cup onions, minced

1 egg, separated

¼ teaspoon salt

Generous dash powdered cloves

Lemon wedge

Carbohydrates	Grams
carrots	22.0
butter	0.2
onions	15.0
egg	0.5
Total	37.7
per serving	9.4

Steam carrots until very tender, about 20 minutes. Melt butter over low heat and cook onion until tender. Preheat oven to 350°F. Puree carrots in blender or potato ricer (Foley mill). Add egg yolk and beat until smooth. In a small bowl, beat egg white until stiff, then fold into carrot mixture. Add salt and cloves. Turn mixture into buttered 5 x 9-inch glass loaf pan and bake 20 to 25 minutes. Serve hot with a lemon wedge. Serves 4.

Jell Treat

1 cup hot water

2 heaping teaspoons Dacopa[22]

1 heaping tablespoon unflavored gelatin

Ice cubes

Fake Cream for topping (optional) (see page 179)

Carbohydrates	Grams
.........................negligible	

Make a jell by mixing hot water, Dacopa (see Note below), and gelatin in the blender at low speed. Drop ice cubes one at a time into the blender, while continuing to blend until jelled. Serve with or without Fake Cream. Serves 2 or 3.

NOTE: Dahlia tuber coffee substitute or other coffee substitute is made without malt or fruit. Found in health/natural food stores.

Fake Cream

When good quality whipping cream (raw certified or pasteurized with no additives—not Ultra Pasteurized) is unavailable, try this substitute.

1 cup hot (near boiling) pure water

1 rounded tablespoon pure unflavored gelatin (vegetable gelatin, called agar-agar, if you can find it)

1 stick (½ cup) unsalted butter

3 eggs

1 tablespoon pure vanilla extract (see Note below)

Ice cubes

Carbohydrates	Grams
butter	0.8
eggs	1.5
Total	2.3

Pour water into blender. Slowly add gelatin and blend at low speed. Add butter, eggs, and vanilla extract, continuing to blend. As blender whirs, add ice cubes one at a time through the inner lid until the mixture jells. Makes a quart of Fake Cream.

Variations: Use as a base for eggnog or as a cereal topping. Drop frozen berries into the mixture, instead of ice cubes, to make an instant fruit ice cream.

NOTE: Bickford's pure extracts are made from herbs, foods, and spices in a corn oil base. Find them in natural food stores.

Sweet Potato Soufflé

3 small sweet potatoes

3 eggs, separated

¼ cup pure water, boiling

1 tablespoon unflavored gelatin

1 teaspoon pumpkin pie spice mix

½ cup whipped cream or Fake Cream (see page 179)

Carbohydrates	Grams
sweet potatoes	111.0
eggs	1.5
gelatin	0.0
spice	0.5
Total	113.0
per serving	18.8

Steam sweet potatoes and blend, rice, or mash to produce about 2 cups pulp. Separate eggs. Place water in blender, turn on low speed, and add gelatin. Gradually add egg yolks, pumpkin pie spice, and sweet potato pulp while continuing to blend into puree. Chill. It will form a firm custard. Serve in sherbet glasses. Top with whipped cream or Fake Cream. Makes six ½-cup servings.

Beef Jerky

The marinades given for the beef and lamb jerky are delicious additions to many foods.

2 pounds beef, sliced very thin (ask your butcher to do this for you)

4 cloves garlic (use your garlic crusher, or mince with sharp knife)

Juice of 1 lemon

1 teaspoon Celtic sea salt

2 drops liquid stevia extract

1 hot pepper, minced (optional)

Carbohydrates	Grams
beef	0.0
garlic	3.6
lemon	3.0
Celtic sea salt	0.0
stevia	0.0
Total	6.6

Arrange meat slices on your dehydrator trays. Mix the remaining ingredients in a small bowl. Spoon the mixture over thin meat slices and dehydrate at 98°F until crisp (this takes less than 24 hours in my kitchen). Store in airtight containers in the freezer or refrigerator, or some other cool place for a short time.

Lamb Jerky

2 pounds lamb (boneless leg), sliced very thin

¼ cup packed mint leaves

1 teaspoon Celtic sea salt

Juice of 1 lemon

2 drops liquid stevia

Carbohydrates	Grams
lamb	0
mint	unknown
Celtic sea salt	0
lemon	3
stevia	0
Total	3

Arrange meat slices on your dehydrator trays. Blend the rest of the ingredients. Spoon this blended mixture over lamb slices and dehydrate at 98°F until crisp. This usually takes a day and a half in my kitchen, as I cannot get the lamb slices as thin as the beef. Your butcher can help with this slicing.

Salmon Jerky

1 teaspoon ginger root,
freshly grated

1 tablespoon Bragg's aminos

2 pounds fresh salmon, thinly
sliced (as for sashimi)

Carbohydrates	Grams
salmon ....unknown
ginger root ....2.6 per ounce

Mix ginger root and aminos. Gently spoon marinade over salmon slices arranged on dehydrator trays. Dehydrate at 98°F until crisp (approximately 1 to 2 days).

Martine's Vegetable Crackers

2 large tomatoes, chopped

2 carrots, chopped

1 or 2 stalks celery, chopped

1 small head or 2 crowns broccoli, chopped

2 cloves garlic

1 small jicama or several pieces Jerusalem artichoke, chopped

1 beet, chopped

Celtic sea salt to taste

Carbohydrates	Grams
tomatoes	6.0
carrots	1.4
celery	4.0
broccoli	10.0
garlic	1.8
jicama	16.7
beet	10.0
Celtic sea salt	0.0
Total	50.0

Blend or food process all ingredients to a puree consistency. Spread on plastic sheets in your dehydrator trays. Dehydrate 1 to 2 days until crisp and crunchy. Break into cracker-size pieces and store in airtight container.

Treated Almonds

Fresh almonds

Carbohydrates	Grams
almonds ....28 per cup	

Soak almonds overnight, then drain and rinse at least 3 times each day until there is a "nubbin" bulge of a sprout (after about 2 days). Remove any bran coating, spread nuts on your dehydrator trays, and dry at 98°F until crispy.

Whipped Almond Butter

For one:

¼ pound butter

1½ tablespoons water

¾ teaspoon almond extract

2 tablespoons chopped almonds

Carbohydrates	Grams
butter............................0.8	
almond extract 0.0	
almonds 3.5	
per serving 4.5	

For a party:

1 pound good quality butter

2 tablespoons cold pure water

1 tablespoon almond extract

½ cup finely chopped, treated almonds

Let the butter warm to room temperature. Whip, blend, or process butter, water, and almond extract until light and fluffy. Add chopped almonds and mix well. Chill and serve.

Rice Popovers

4 eggs

1 cup water

¼ teaspoon kelp powder

Few drops stevia liquid extract
(start with 7 drops)

1 cup brown rice flour

2 teaspoons coconut butter

Carbohydrates	Grams
eggs	2.0
kelp powder	unknown
stevia	0.0
brown rice flour	85.0
coconut butter	unknown

Add ½ cup water, kelp, stevia, and rice flour to eggs beaten in your blender. When smooth, blend in the other ½ cup water and the coconut butter. Oil popover pan or Pyrex custard cups with additional coconut butter and pour batter to half fill cups. Once batter is in the oven, do not peek while baking! Bake at 450°F for 15 minutes, then turn heat down to 350°F for 30 minutes longer. Makes 6 large or 12 smaller popovers—approximately 87 carbohydrate grams per recipe. Divide by number of popovers for individual carbohydrate count.

BEVERAGES

There is no universal agreement as to what type of potable water is best, but most experts agree that ordinarily tap water should be avoided. In the recipes, we refer both to cooking and drinking water, and suggest the use of spring, purified, filtered water, or water treated by reverse osmosis. For the average person the total daily quantity should be from six to eight glasses, spaced throughout the day.

One of the most important books to come to our attention recently is *Your Body's Many Cries for Water* by F. Batmanghelidj, M.D., which tells us that many modern health symptoms are indications of unrecognized dehydration and encourages us to approach these symptoms (body signals) by drinking more pure water.

Water from the steamer pot contains minerals leached from cooking. This liquid can be saved for broths rather than thrown away.

Sparkling waters, especially mineral waters, are enjoyable with a twist of lemon or lime.

Herb teas are popular but may contain molds. Their use depends on individual tolerances. Many use pau d'arco (taheebo) tea. It is reported to have antifungal properties. Other teas with similar qualities include chamomile, bergamot, hyssop, alfalfa, angelica root, and lemon grass.

Avoid coffee, nonherbal tea, and artificially sweetened beverages. Try the beverages in this cookbook and experiment on your own.

Eggnog

This is an ideal beverage to take with any vitamin or mineral powders your doctor has prescribed.

1 egg

¼ cup Fake Cream (see page 179) or 1 tablespoon cream

3 tablespoons water

Carbohydrates	Grams
egg	0.5
Fake Cream	0.1
Total	0.6

Blend all ingredients quickly.

Variation: For a brisk flavor, add 4 fresh mint leaves.

Lemon-Cinnamon Tea

2 sticks cinnamon

2 cups water

Juice and peel of ½ lemon

Carbohydrates	Grams
lemon juice and peel	2.9
per serving	0.7

Place cinnamon in water in saucepan and cook over low heat. After steeping about 15 minutes, add the juice and peel of lemon. Steep without heat, but covered, another 5 minutes. Serves 4.

Lemon Trilogy Tea

1 teaspoon each lemon grass,
lemon balm, and lemon verbena

1 quart water

Carbohydrates	Grams
..........................negligible	

Prepare as herb tea or steeped tea.

Variations: If you have a lemon tree, use 1 or 2 leaves from it as well. A blossom or two from any citrus tree adds greatly to the fragrance of this brew.

Lemonade

Juice of ½ lemon

8-ounce glass of pure water

3 to 7 drops liquid stevia
extract

Carbohydrates	Grams
lemon juice .... 1 (per teaspoon)	
stevia 0	
Total 1	

Add lemon juice to glass of water. Add stevia—let your taste
buds be your guide for sweetener. Enjoy!

Mint-Flavored Cafe

This was grandmother's remedy for
disturbed digestion. Many a stom-
achache was feigned to obtain the
remedy!

Carbohydrates	Grams
.... negligible	

1 cup dandelion or chicory tea

2 to 4 drops peppermint oil

Pour a cup of boiling water over a tablespoon of dandelion or
chicory tea or a handful of fresh leaves, cover tightly, and steep
for 10 to 20 minutes. Add peppermint and stir.

Peppermint Tea

1 handful mint leaves or
½ cup dried mint leaves

1 quart water

Carbohydrates	Grams
.........................negligible	

Chop a handful of mint leaves and cover with 1 quart hot water, or take ¼ cup dried mint leaves and soak 6 hours in a quart of water. Strain. Heat to serving temperature, if desired.

Variation: Place either fresh or dried mint and water in the blender and whirl, then strain. Serves 4.

Sparkling Herb Tea

2 tablespoons dried herbs, or ⅓ cup fresh

1 quart pure water

Ice cubes made with pure water

Carbohydrates	Grams
.........................negligible	

1 quart sparkling water

Lemon slices (optional)

Add any favorite herbs or combination of herbs to water and simmer in a covered pot for 20 minutes. Let tea cool to room temperature. Pour into quart jar, cover and chill 1 to 2 hours. Put ice cubes in glasses. Fill glasses half full with tea, and the remainder with sparkling water. Drop 1 lemon slice into each glass. Makes eight 8-ounce servings.

Eating Out

Prepare your own food as much as possible. Use frozen leftovers you have prepared for emergencies when pressed for time. A tempting alternative to dining out is to treat yourself to an expensive cut of meat or fish you ordinarily would not buy and prepare it at home to accompany your favorite vegetables.

Often, dining out is unavoidable. When this occurs, make the best of it if you aren't going to cheat. It is hoped that you will be dining at a good restaurant where food is prepared fresh daily on the premises. Choose plain foods. Avoid those with sauces that are apt to contain sugar and vinegar. If they are tasty, you are tempted to overeat. Order the foods to which you have become accustomed, such as prime rib, roast or baked chicken, poached or broiled fish. Avoid charcoal-grilled foods and rolled deli meats. Share a baked potato with a friend.

Order Perrier with a wedge of lime and make it a festive occasion. Request a vegetable relish plate, try vegetable dishes à la carte, or select a homemade clear (not cream) soup with vegetables.

Sip a cup of herbal tea (carry your own tea bag) or simply flavor a cup of steaming hot water with lemon. Above all, make the event enjoyable.

A Menu Sampler

BREAKFAST

Measure servings carefully since it is difficult to gauge ¼-cup size portions initially. Take care to consult the carbohydrate charts if in doubt. Your basic breakfast consists of 1 part protein, 1 part starch, and 5 parts vegetables. Some suggested substitutes for cereals in the following menus are:

- Freshly ground cream of rye, oats, rice
- Steamed whole grain wheat, barley, millet, oats
- Sweet potato or other tuber pancakes

A "hurry-up" breakfast may include:
- Eggnog
- Sweet potato muffin
- Choice of 4 raw vegetables

BREAKFAST I

1 serving flaxseed cereal
with ⅛ cup heavy cream

¼ cup portions each of:
  - broiled fish
  - steamed chard
  - steamed peas
  - raw carrot
  - raw celery
  - raw tomato

BREAKFAST II

1 serving cream of grain
(wheat) cereal with butter

Broiled lamb kidneys

¼ cup portion each of:
  - steamed asparagus
  - steamed beets
  - raw watercress
  - raw cucumber
  - raw bell pepper

BREAKFAST III

1 serving psyllium
seed cereal

⅛ cup heavy cream

Spanish omelet,
1 serving

BREAKFAST IV

1 serving steamed whole grain
rye cereal

¼ cup portions each of:

- poached egg on steamed
  beet greens
- steamed beets
- raw celery
- raw zucchini and
  broccoli florets

BREAKFAST V

1 serving oat bran cereal
with heavy cream

¼ cup portion each of:

- broiled steak
- steamed celery with
  edible pea pods
- raw turnip slices,
  parsley sprigs, and
  cherry tomatoes

BREAKFAST VI

¼ of oat bran waffle
and butter

¼ cup portion each of:

- lamb sausage
- steamed broccoli
  and celery
- raw carrots, radishes,
  and lettuce

Lunch

Luncheon ideas include soups or stews, salads, raw vegetables with dips, or cooked vegetables. Some cold cooked meats, fish, or fowl are tasty. These, as well as your favorite egg dishes, can be served steaming hot.

Lunch I	Lunch II
turkey hash	Italian fish stew
salad	salad

Lunch III	Lunch IV
broiled chicken	tostadas
Caesar salad	raw vegetables

Lunch V	Lunch VI
steak salad	fish salad
mug of hot broth	mug of hot mint tea

Remember to use ¼-cup servings except when the dish consists of a mixture. Then multiply the ¼ cup by the vegetables and protein in the recipe. Repeat the process for dinners.

DINNER

DINNER I
roast turkey and gravy
stovetop holiday dressing
green salad

DINNER II
lamb kabobs
mint-pea salad

DINNER III
cooked tongue
steamed broccoli
assorted raw vegetables

DINNER IV
poached fish
asparagus and hollandaise sauce
kasha
coleslaw

DINNER V
broiled beefsteak
crowned eggplant
carrot-cabbage salad

DINNER VI
vegetable-beef soup
millet muffin
assorted raw vegetables

DINNER VII
fish in butter-ginger sauce
small baked potato
steamed string beans
raw tomato, romaine lettuce, and cucumber
anchovy dressing

Candida Folk Wisdom

Garlic is said to be antifungal. Many people suffering from *Candida* claim to feel better when using more garlic than the ordinary amount used as spicy seasoning. The simple way to extract garlic oil for concentrated use is with alcohol such as vodka.

Ingredients:
   ½ pound garlic cloves, peeled
   1 bottle (fifth or quart) vodka or gin

Place the garlic cloves in the blender with 1 cup alcohol. Blend the mixture until it becomes mush. Add a second cup of alcohol and blend. Pour into a quart jar. Rinse the blender with ⅛ cup alcohol and add this to the jar. Cap the jar with a firm-sealing lid that cannot leak. Shake the jar daily just long enough to mix well. Repeat this procedure for 10 days. Each day thereafter check the jar for about 1 inch of garlic oil rising to the top. Remove the oil by gently skimming or pouring. Don't use any of the mash sediment.

Collect the oil in an eye-dropper bottle and use as seasoning or external remedy. It is delicious blended into softened butter to top vegetables, or in the salad dressing. Each time oil is removed, add a little alcohol to the jar. When no more oil rises, discard the mush and make a new batch.

Taheebo or Pau d'Arco Tea

This tea has apparently helped many *Candida* patients. The tea is made from inner tree bark and imported from South America. It is brewed as follows:

>   1 heaping tablespoon tea or the
>   contents of three tea bags,
>   emptied into pot
>
>   1 quart water

Add the water to the tea and simmer on the lowest heat possible for at least half an hour. Allow the liquid to cool and pour into a storage jar with a tight-sealing lid. Refrigerate, and sip the chilled tea as desired. Adjust the recipe to make enough to be completely consumed in two days.

Foods for the Yeast-Sensitive to Avoid*

Yeast is found in all manufactured citric acid and in most fruits; in vinegar, which is made of fermented wines; and in ciders from such fruits as grapes, pears, apples, and some herbs. Vinegar is used as a preservative for mustard, catsup, olives, mayonnaise, many dressings, pickles, horseradish, spices, soy sauce, Worcestershire sauce, and dried fruits. Canned or frozen fruit juices contain yeast; only hand-squeezed and fresh juices are yeast-free. Fruit and fruit products that are canned commercially have a higher yeast content than those that are canned at home. Melons (especially cantaloupe) and oranges are loaded with molds and yeast on the outside skins. Fruits should be peeled, not cut into, because in the motion of cutting through the skin with a knife, the meat of the fruit is contaminated.

Mushrooms and cheeses of all kinds contain or actually are specific types of molds or yeasts; for instance, Roquefort cheese contains the mold *Penicillium roqueforti*. Other yeast-containing milk products are buttermilk, sour cream, cream

---

* This information is used with the kind permission of John A. Henderson, M.D., E.N.T., *Surgery and Allergy*, San Diego, California, 1984.

cheese, ricotta cheese, ice creams, powdered milks, and milk itself.

Tea, pepper, coffee, coffee substitutes, many spices, and tobacco acquire molds or yeast in their drying processes. Leftovers from a previous meal should be frozen for future use, as they will become mold-containing within twenty-four hours. Brown spots on any food are yeasts and molds that have begun their job of breaking down that food's nutrients for their own survival. Vitamins, such as the B-complex thiamine, niacin, and riboflavin, are usually yeast-grown, although it is possible to obtain them with a brown rice base, yeast-free. Antibiotics such as penicillin, mycin drugs, tetracyclines, linococin, and chloromycetin are derived from mold cultures.

Malt is used as a flavoring and coloring agent; it is the major ingredient of beer, ale, and malt liquors, as well as some nonalcoholic products. Malt is a sprouted grain, easily fermented, and produces the enzyme diastase, important in the development of grain liquors. Most dry breakfast cereals contain malt or malt extract—Grape-Nuts is exceptionally high in malt content.

Other foods which encourage *Candida albicans* are baked goods, breads, biscuits, pancake mixes, soda crackers, and any other foods requiring the use of baker's yeast. Ice cream, candy, malted milk drinks, and soda fountain drinks contain sugar yeast.

Carbohydrates and Calories

This list has been abbreviated to refer to the antifungal diet. Some additional foods to augment the diet have been added. Care should be taken, as the body chemistry improves and symptoms become less severe, to experiment with caution.

The figures have been drawn from:

    Nutritive Value of Foods, Science and Education Administration, Home and Garden Bulletin Number 72.

    Composition of Foods, Agriculture Handbook Number 8, Agricultural Research Service, U.S.D.A.

For further information on expanded dietary needs consult:

    Nutrition Almanac, Nutrition Search Inc. New York: McGraw-Hill.

    Composition and Facts about Foods, Ford Heritage, Health Research, P.O. Box 70, Mokelumne Hill, CA 95245.

Where figures are not available from the U.S. Government publications, the numbers given are approximate.

    Note: Foods noted with an asterisk are those to be added judiciously to the diet when tolerated.

Food	Portion	Carbs (Grams)	Calories
*almonds	¼ cup	6.9	
	1 cup	27.7	600
*arrowroot	1 cup	112.0	
	1 T	7.0	
artichoke, globe	1 average size	10.6	44
artichoke, Jerusalem	½ cup	16.7	50
asparagus	1 cup	5.0	30
avocado	1	12.6	334
baking powder	1 t	2.0	5
	1T	7.0	
bamboo shoots	4 spears	2.0	10
barley	¼ cup	19.0	150
beans			
*black-eyed peas	1 cup	35.0	190
*garbanzos	1 cup dry	122.0	720
	1 cup cooked	60.0	360
green snap, cooked	½ cup	4.0	25
raw	1 cup	7.0	30
*kidney, cooked	1 cup	42.0	238
*lima	1 cup	35.0	190
*pinto, cooked	1 cup	60.5	330

Food	Portion	Carbs (Grams)	Calories
beets			
cooked, whole	2 (2")	7.0	30
cooked, sliced or diced	1 cup	13.5	55
beverages			
carbonated water		0	0
club soda		0	0
Perrier	1 bottle	0	0
*blackberries	1 cup	19.0	85
*blueberries	1 cup	22.0	90
bok choy, cooked	1 cup	4.0	25
raw	1 cup	7.0	40
broccoli, cooked	1 cup	7.0	40
brussels sprouts, cooked	1 cup	10.0	55
*bulgur, cooked	1 cup	85.0	420
dry	1 cup	129.0	602
butter, ¼ pound	½ cup	0.8	814
cabbage			
cooked	1 cup	6.0	30
Chinese	1 cup	2.0	10
raw, shredded (red and white)	1 cup	5.0	20
cacciatore sauce	1 cup	40.0	

Food	Portion	Carbs (Grams)	Calories
carbonated water		0	0
carob	½ cup	58.4	112
	1 T	7.3	16
carrot, cooked	1 cup	11.0	50
grated	1 cup	11.0	45
raw	7¼ x ⅛"	7.0	30
cauliflower	1 cup	6.0	31
celeriac	½ cup	8.5	40
celery, 1 stalk	8" x 1½"	2.0	5
chopped	1 cup	4.7	
leaves chopped	1 cup	5.0	
chayote, diced	1 cup	5.0	20
chicken livers	1 cup	8.2	
chives	¾ cup	6.0	28
cilantro	½ cup	1.0	
corn, 1 ear	5" x 1¾"	16.0	79
*kernels, cooked	1 cup	31.0	130
corn meal, grits			
*cooked	1 cup	27.0	125
*uncooked	1 cup	90.0	435

Food	Portion	Carbs (Grams)	Calories
cucumber	1¾" x 1	1.0	5
diced	1 cup	3.6	16
dandelion greens, cooked	1 cup	7.0	35
egg, large	1	0.5	80
eggplant, steamed	1 cup	7.4	34
cooked	1 large	18–20	100
endive, raw	1 cup	2.0	10
fish, fowl, meats		0	
garlic	1 clove	0.9	4
ginger root	1 ounce	2.6	
gelatin	1 T	0	25
*grapefruit	half	13.0	50
greens, cooked			
beet	1 cup	5.0	25
collard	1 cup	10.0	65
mustard	1 cup	6.0	30
turnip	1 cup	5.0	30
herbs, most		0	0
horseradish	1 t	0.5	2

Food	Portion	Carbs (Grams)	Calories
jicama	1 cup	25.6	
kale, cooked	1 cup	7.0	45
lemon juice	1 T	1.0	4
*lentils, cooked	1 cup	39.0	210
lettuce			
Boston	5" head	4.0	25
iceberg	6" head	12.5	70
loose-leaf, chopped	1 cup	2.0	10
lime juice	1 cup	22.0	65
mayonnaise	1 cup	2.6	1600
	1 T	0.06	100
millet, cooked	1 cup	56.0	248
dry	1 cup	166.0	746
mustard	1 t	0	5
nuts:			
*Brazil	3 ounces	7.5	400
*filberts	1 cup	19.0	730
*macadamia	½ cup	15.9	691
*pecans	1 cup	17.0	816
*pine nuts	½ cup	12.0	550
*walnuts	1 cup	19.0	780
oat bran	⅓ cup	16.0	110

Food	Portion	Carbs (Grams)	Calories
oatmeal, cooked	1 cup	23.0	130
oils		0	
okra, 3" x ⅝"	10 pods	6.0	30
olives, ripe	3 small, 2 large	0.1	15
onions:			
chopped	1 cup	15.0	65
sliced	1 cup	10.0	45
*papaya, cubed	1 cup	14.0	55
parsley, chopped	1 cup	5.0	trace
parsnips	1 cup	23.0	100
peas, cooked	1 cup	19.0	110
peapods or snowpeas	½ cup	24.0	
peppers, sweet, raw	1	4.9	15
chopped	½ cup	1.9	
potatoes			
*diced	1 cup	25.7	114
*baked	1 8-ounce	33.0	145
*boiled	1 5-ounce	23.0	105
*sweet, baked	1 6½-ounce	37.0	160
boiled	1 6½-ounce	40.0	170

Food	Portion	Carbs (Grams)	Calories
*popcorn, popped	1 cup	5.0	25
*pumpkin seeds	1 cup	21.0	775
radishes, raw	4	1.0	5
*raspberries	1 cup	13.0	55
rice, brown			
cooked	1 cup	37.0	178
raw	1 cup	161.0	744
wild	1 cup	30.0	145
flour	1 cup	85.0	270
rutabaga, cooked	1 cup	15.4	64
sliced, raw	1 cup	13.9	60
rye, whole grain	1 cup	68	330
scallions, chopped	1 cup	8.2	36
sesame seeds	1 cup	26.4	873
shallots, chopped	1 cup	27.2	112
sunflower seeds	1 cup	28.9	812
spinach, chopped			
cooked	1 cup	6.0	40
raw	1 cup	2.0	15

Food	Portion	Carbs (Grams)	Calories
squash, cooked			
summer	1 cup	7.0	30
*winter, mashed	1 cup	32.0	130
*strawberries	1 cup	13.0	55
*taro, tuber	½ cup	24.0	98
tomatoes:			
raw	4 ounces	6.0	25
canned, no citric acid			
fresh, chopped	1 cup	10.0	50
tomato paste	1 T	3.0	13
tortillas, corn	1	13.5	
turnips, diced	1 cup	8.0	35
watercress	1 cup	2.2	
*watermelon	4" x 8" wedge	27.0	110
wheat, whole	1 cup	34.0	85
whipping cream	1 cup	7.0	700–800
zucchini, chopped	1 cup	5.5	

References

1. *C. Orian Truss, M.D., *The Missing Diagnosis* (Birmingham, Alabama: P.O. Box 26508, Birmingham, Alabama 35226, 1983).
2. C. Orian Truss, M.D., "The Role of *Candida Albicans* in Human Illness," *Journal of Orthomolecular Psychiatry* vol. 10, no. 4 (1981).
3. *William G. Crook, M.D., *The Yeast Connection* (Jackson, Tennessee: Professional Books, 1984).
4. *Weston A. Price, D.D.S., *Nutrition and Physical Degeneration* (La Mesa, California: Price-Pottenger Nutrition Foundation, 1997).
5. *Melvin E. Page, D.D.S., and H. Leon Abrams, Jr., *Your Body Is Your Best Doctor* (Los Angeles: Keats Publishing, 1972).
6. **Shirley Lorenzani, Ph.D., article reprints included in Candida Reprints *Candida Albicans, Friend or Foe* (La Mesa, California: Price-Pottenger Nutrition Foundation, 1984).
7. *William G. Crook, M.D., *The Yeast Connection*.
8. James Beard, *The Theory and Practice of Good Cooking* (New York: Alfred A. Knopf, 1977).

---

*Items noted may be ordered from the Price-Pottenger Nutrition Foundation, P.O. Box 2614, La Mesa, California 91943.

**Shirley Lorenzani, Ph.D., Cassette Tapes, Sets I and II (La Mesa, Calif.: Price-Pottenger Nutrition Foundation, 1978).

9. Clara Felix, *The Felix Letter* (Berkeley, California, P.O. Box 7094, 94754, 1983): vol. 16.
10. Jeffrey Bland, Ph.D., *Digestive Enzymes*, (Los Angeles: Keats Publishing, 1983). James W. Anderson, M.D., Veterans Administration Medical Center, Lexington, KY 40511, *The American Journal of Clinical Nutrition* 34 (May 1981).
11. *Pat Connolly, *Guide to Living Foods* (La Mesa, California: Price-Pottenger Nutrition Foundation, 1978).
12. Brenner Stainless Steel, 1741 North Ivar, Office 90028, Suite 111, or P.O. Box 549, Hollywood, California 90078.
13. Adelle Davis, *Let's Cook It Right* (New York: New American Library, 1970).
14. *Melvin E. Page, D.D.S., and H. Leon Abrams, Jr., *Your Body Is Your Best Doctor.* (La Mesa, California: Price-Pottenger Foundation).
15. Adelle Davis, *Let's Cook It Right*.
16. Beatrice Trum Hunter, *The Natural Foods Primer* (New York: Simon and Schuster, 1972).
17. James Beard, *Theory and Practice of Good Cooking*.
18. James Beard, *Fish Cookery* (New York: Warner Books, 1967).
19. Irma S. Rombauer and Marion Rombauer Becker, *Joy of Cooking* (Indianapolis: Bobbs Merrill, 1967).
20. *Francis M. Pottenger Jr., M.D., *Pottenger's Cats* (La Mesa, California: Price-Pottenger Nutrition Foundation, 1983).
21. James Beard, *Theory and Practice of Good Cooking*.
22. Essene Bread, made of sprouted grains and yeast-free ingredients, can be found in your health food store or ordered from distributors: on the West Coast, California Natural Foods Products, Mateca, California 95336; East Coast, Stowmills, P.O. Box 816, Brattleboro, Vermont 05301.

Resources

ORGANIZATIONS

Candida & Disbiosis Information Foundation
P.O. Box JF
College Station, Texas 77841
(409) 694-8687

William Crook's Foundation
International Health Foundation
P. O. Box 3494
Jackson, Tennessee 38303

BOOKS

Batmanghelidj, F. *Your Body's Many Cries for Water.* Falls Church, Va.: Global Health Solutions, 1995.

Crook, William G. *The Yeast Connection Handbook.* Jackson, Tenn.: Professional Books Inc., 1997.

Ingram, Cass. *Supermarket Remedies.* Buffalo Grove, Ill.: Knowledge House, 1998.

Lorenzani, Shirley. *Candida: A 21st Century Disease.* Los Angeles Kcats Publishing, 1986.

Pottenger, Francis Marion, Jr. *Pottenger's Cats.* San Diego, Calif.: Price Pottenger Nutrition Foundation, 1983.

Price, Weston A. *Nutrition and Physical Degeneration*. Los Angeles: Keats Publishing, 1997.

Tips, Jack. *The ProVita Plan*. Austin, Tex.: Apple A Day Press, 1992.

Truss, C. Orian. *The Missing Diagnosis*. Birmingham, Ala.: self-published, 1983.

Index